THE POWER OF TWO

THE POWER OF TWO

OF TWO

How Smart Companies Create Win–Win Customer–Supplier
Partnerships that Outperform the Competition

Carlos Cordón
and
Thomas E. Vollmann

First published 2008 by
PALGRAVE MACMILLAN
Houndmills, Basingstoke, Hampshire RG21 6XS and
175 Fifth Avenue, New York, N.Y. 10010

Companies and representatives throughout the world

PALGRAVE MACMILLAN is the global academic imprint of the Palgrave
Macmillan division of St. Martin's Press, LLC and of Palgrave Macmillan Ltd.
Macmillan® is a registered trademark in the United States, United Kingdom
and other countries. Palgrave is a registered trademark in the European
Union and other countries.

ISBN-13: 978–0–230–21888–8
ISBN-10: 0–230–21888–1

This book is printed on paper suitable for recycling and made from fully
managed and sustained forest sources. Logging, pulping and manufacturing
processes are expected to conform to the environmental regulations of the
country of origin.

A catalogue record for this book is available from the British Library.

A catalog record for this book is available from the Library of Congress.

10 9 8 7 6 5 4 3 2 1
17 16 15 14 13 12 11 10 09 08

Printed and bound in China

To la tia Laura y el tio Josemari

In memory of Archie Kvaal

With love to Minerva and Tani

CONTENTS

List of figures and tables   xi

Acknowledgments   xiii

Case studies   xv

About the authors   xvii

Introduction   I

Chapter I   **Picking ten partners**   **9**
               Why is ten the magic number?   I2
               The new game   I6
               Smarter buying and selling   22
               So what?   26

Chapter 2   **Mastering the four stages of collaboration**   **27**
               Stage I: flawless execution   29
               Stage 2: total cost of ownership   32
               Stage 3: value/cost   36
               Stage 4: strategic alignment   39
               Governance   42
               So what?   44

Chapter 3   **Restructuring procurement**   **47**
               Leveraging the collaborative segment   48
               Separating the sheep from the goats   51
               Be the most attractive customer   55

	Setting the improvement agenda	59
	So what?	66
Chapter 4	**Selling the way your customers *want to buy***	**69**
	Business-to-business selling is different	70
	Selling to customer segmentation models	76
	Key account management	81
	When customers change the game	85
	So what?	88
Chapter 5	**Choosing your battles wisely**	**91**
	Proactive sales leadership	94
	Key sales elements	96
	Deploying your sales resources	102
	Being the most attractive supplier	104
	Delivering what customers need	107
	So what?	110
Chapter 6	**Developing pairs of aces**	**113**
	Success is easily killed	113
	Keeping the faith	117
	Negotiation II	120
	It takes two to tango	123
	A winning journey	129
	So what?	134
Chapter 7	**Building the future**	**137**
	The Rubik's cube of customer–supplier partnerships	138
	Driving the procurement agenda	146
	Pushing sales and marketing	151
	Making it all work	157
	So what?	160
Chapter 8	**Changing two at a time**	**163**
	From one-sided to two-sided change	163
	From key account management to key collaboration management	171
	Where is the win–win?	176
	So what?	178

Chapter 9   **Harnessing the power of two**   **181**
Driving from procurement   181
Driving from sales   184
So what?   186

Bibliography   *187*

Index   *191*

Figures and tables

Figures

1.1	Procurement evolution	13
1.2	Typical mix of collaborative relationships	17
1.3	Super-supplier collaboration	18
2.1	The four stages of collaboration	29
2.2	Progressive collaboration stages	39
3.1	Supplier segmentation	52
3.2	Nokia's supplier matrix	54
3.3	Motivation/pressure versus performance	63
4.1	Segmentation of suppliers from a purchasing point of view	76
4.2	A customer–supplier relationship based on more than price	80
5.1	Procurement deployment	92
5.2	Product sourcing strategy	92
6.1	Leading and lagging indicators	116
6.2	Changing customer and supplier positioning	121
6.3	The hierarchy of supply chain metrics	124
6.4	The two-sided staircase model for joint improvement	125
6.5	Extending lean with dyads: the BPR/IT challenge	128
7.1	The Rubik's cube of customer–supplier partnerships	138
8.1	The change management model	165
8.2	Longitudinal versus lateral growth	174

Table

4.1   New sales realities   72

Acknowledgments

We would like to thank all of those who generously gave their time and insights to help us write this book. In addition to those who helped in the case studies listed below, we are indebted to the following organizations and people:

- ABB, especially Dan Ahern, Frank Dugan, and Oliver Riemenschneider
- Bombardier Transport, especially Andre Navarri, Pierre Attendu, Charles O'Donnell, Dr. Falk Mehdorn, and Michel Van Lierde
- Caterpillar, especially Paul Wroblewski and Tom Sandborg
- Knorr-Bremse, especially Heinz Herman Thiele, Dr. Frank Gropengiesser, and Mark Cleobury
- IMD colleagues, especially Corey Billington, Joe DiStefano, Bill Fischer, Winter Nie, Phil Rosenweig, Ralf Seifert, and Paul Strebel
- special thanks to IMD President Peter Lorange, and Vice-President Jim Ellert for their ongoing support and encouragement
- several people who have contributed to our thinking: Luc Volatier, Jussi Hekkila, Alan Hutchison, Chris Ellegaard, Kim Hald, and Dave Nelson
- and finally to someone who has played a key role in our work for several years: Henrik Eklund.

We have also learnt a great deal through our case writing activities, which play a major role in our work with executives here at IMD. The following are some of the key cases and the lessons exemplified from them—any of these can be obtained from IMD:

- ABB and Caterpillar: transforming key account management.
- Dupont: debunking the role of core competencies in outsourcing.
- Freqon: mapping relationships between a customer and supplier over more than ten years.
- Hewlett-Packard: selecting and developing an EMS (electronic manufacturing services) supplier.
- Mabe Estaufas: squeezing suppliers can be counter-productive in the long run.
- Nokia Supply Line Management: a fast response to fix a broken supply chain.
- Numico: working with a creative supplier to develop new products.
- Philips Consumer Electronics: rapid response to major retail customers.
- Skanska & Rockwool: making joint costs visible so they can be collaboratively reduced.
- TeStrake: working jointly in new product development at the technical specifications stage.
- Thomas Medical Systems: developing and implementing outsourcing policies.
- Unichema: why "flawless execution" is a prerequisite to customer partnerships.
- Victoria's Secret: implementing a council of suppliers.

Carlos Cordón is Professor of Manufacturing Management at IMD. He is Spanish, and has special interests in supply/demand chain management, speed-based management, project management, and outsourcing. He is a consultant to multinational companies in industries including electronics, food, chemicals, pharmaceuticals, and cars. He has won various prizes for his cases and articles on supply chain management, outsourcing, and procurement.

Thomas Vollmann is an American who has spent the past 20 years in Europe. He is Professor (Emeritus) of Manufacturing Management at IMD. His areas of special interest are manufacturing planning and control, performance measurement, supply chain management, and procurement. He is a consultant to numerous companies in manufacturing, procurement, and demand chain management, and a lecturer in executive development programs throughout the world. Professor Vollmann is the author/co-author of 12 books, over 50 case studies (8 of which have won awards), and approximately 100 journal articles.

Introduction

In the course of our work as professors and consultants we were struck by a simple observation. We noticed that the best performing companies enjoy special relationships with a few key suppliers and customers.

Managers at Honda, for example, talk about "super suppliers"— a small group of companies with which the company enjoys a special relationship. The more we looked, the more we realized that a similar approach was evident at other firms that outperformed their industries. Over time, we developed a simple shorthand term to describe the impact of these deep relationships—we call it the "power of two".

The power of two presents what we see as the best way for your company to increase its competitive advantage. By forming close collaborative relationships with a small set of customers and suppliers, you can achieve cost breakthroughs, increase your market share, achieve significant top-line growth, and create competencies that cannot be copied.

The ideas presented here are the result of several years of research, exploring them with thousands of executives at IMD and working as consultants to firms implementing the concepts. Putting the plan into action requires you to make some difficult changes in your company—as well as in the companies of key customers and suppliers. But the payoffs are significant and achievable. Here are a few examples:

- Toyota has a distinct cost advantage over its US competitors. At least $1,000 per vehicle is derived from lower-cost components. This has been achieved through collaborative efforts in which

Toyota and key suppliers have jointly taken out unnecessary costs and jointly added value. The results were not achieved by the usual cost-cutting method of tougher negotiating techniques.

- ABB, the Swedish-Swiss engineering giant, is increasing its top-line growth by focusing on key accounts, whose revenue has grown significantly faster than that of the company's regular business. This result has also been achieved through collaborative efforts: Here the focus is on new ways to jointly develop global account management with carefully selected customers.

- Hewlett-Packard has developed a special relationship with Canon over many years. This collaboration has enabled many joint activities that have been true win–win. An HP executive stated that he feels this relationship is perhaps HP's single most important asset.

- Bombardier Transport (BT), the Montreal-based train manufacturer, has recently developed collaborative partnerships with ten suppliers. Working jointly, they have been able to support a significant increase in BT's market share. BT can bid with aggressive prices, it can deliver at those prices, and BT and the suppliers can still make good returns.

This book describes these and many other examples in which a carefully chosen customer and supplier have developed powerful collaborative relations. We call these relationships *"pairs of aces."* It is the collaborative and symbiotic nature of the pairs of aces relationship that unlocks the phenomenon we call the power of two.

In each case, the customer and the supplier have recognized their need to jointly overhaul the way they do business: taking out unnecessary work, reducing any cost that is borne by either of them, creating greater value, and capitalizing on a new strategic relationship. This is within reach: not with all of a company's customers or suppliers, of course, but with a carefully chosen few. These are the relationships in which the necessary trust can be established, and mechanisms developed to resolve the inevitable differences in opinions and perceptions, so that win–win becomes a clearly shared objective.

The book maps out the journey which enables smart companies to create win–win relationships to outperform the competition.

Chapter 1, Picking ten partners, focuses on the massive improvements a few companies already enjoy through working closely with their suppliers and customers. Our experience indicates that ten represents a reasonable upper limit on how many of these special relationships a company can develop. Any company that says it is partnering with 100 suppliers or customers needs to understand that these cannot be serious partnerships. Each true partnership requires a major investment of time, money, and energy. Success requires very careful selection and a joint commitment: It is the customer and the supplier that must both change, invest in the partnership, address the inevitable resistance in their companies, and continually move ahead. A partnership is not real unless it has an aggressive improvement agenda.

- The key message here is that it is only with a limited number of customers and/or suppliers that one can develop the necessary joint competencies and overcome classic zero-sum thinking.

Chapter 2, Mastering the four stages of collaboration, provides a broad roadmap for collaboration, the goals to be attained at each stage, the changes required to achieve them, and the payoffs that should be expected. It is critical that both customer and supplier see this roadmap as the route to be traveled, the payoffs that each of them should demand for the efforts, and not underestimate the pain that must be incurred.

The first stage, flawless execution, involves the changes both customer and supplier must make to ensure on-time deliveries, customer schedule performance excellence, and quality perfection. It is critical to not assume this to only be the responsibility of the supplier.

The second stage, total cost of ownership, focuses both companies' energies to identify any cost in either firm that might be eliminated or sharply reduced through collaborative efforts.

The third stage, value/cost optimization, recognizes explicitly that the numerator in this ratio may well be more important than the denominator. The two firms need to jointly work on issues such as new product development, joint efforts to increase customer top-line growth, and developing greater speed for mutual advantage.

Finally, stage four deals with strategic alignment: Finding ways for the customer and supplier to see a collective future and developing joint competencies that are impossible for others to duplicate.

- The key message is that developing the pair of aces relationship is a long and continuous process, one that needs constant care and feeding as well as new challenges, new joint projects, and new payoffs to both parties.

Chapter 3, Restructuring procurement, focuses on the changes needed in procurement. We start by coming back to the upper limit of ten true partners; this mandates a drastic segmentation of the supplier base. Companies should continue to treat the large proportion of their suppliers in the classic combative way: playing one against another, tough negotiations, etc. A smaller portion should be collaborative and provide the pool from which to develop pairs of aces. Win–win is a key mandate for collaborative procurement; it is essential that the customer be well aware of the key supplier's goals and helps it achieve them. A basic concept is to have the smartest suppliers view you as the most attractive customer, and we offer ten rules for how to be irresistibly attractive.

- Here, we face the classic link between strategy and choice: You can only truly work with a small subset of customers and/or suppliers. Not all choices are possible because of past relationships and because zero-sum games are all too likely to occur.

Chapter 4, Selling the way your customers want to buy, moves us from buying to selling. The primary message here is to understand state-of-the-art buying practices, and how these strongly influence the ways you as a supplier need to behave. Many procurement people understand "reverse marketing" and are trained to be what we call "rottweiler" purchasing agents, with no opportunity or reason to discuss more than your price and how you are to reduce it.

You as a supplier need to know how each customer has categorized you (in what segment, with what treatment). You need to know how to play in each segment, when to say no, and how you might be able to change the game you are playing (move into a different segment). Finally, Chapter 4 introduces the ways key account management might influence the way you are able to sell, and what you need to have from the customer to make it work.

- The key message now is that you must not be naïve about the ease of changing classic buying approaches by your customers. Some will never change, and you need to guard against expressions of partnership that are only new negotiation tactics.

Chapter 5, Choosing your battles wisely, builds on Chapter 4 but shifts to a much more proactive approach. Your salespeople might well be too timid. You need to identify those customers where joint efforts could produce breakthrough results, and then determine a plan of attack in each case that might be feasible. Deciding what is feasible includes analysis of how the customer operates. If it suffers from the "country disease"—that is, all buying decisions made on a decentralized basis—it will in fact be very difficult to achieve joint synergistic benefits. In many cases, success involves expanding the bundle of goods and services provided, systems/solutions selling, and moving up the value chain. But fundamentally, you need your smart customers to see you as attractive, and we offer ten rules for how to make that happen.

- Here we advocate a proactive approach as a supplier. But, you need to understand what doing so implies for the selected customers—as well as for *your* firm.

Chapter 6, Developing pairs of aces, shifts from the "what" and the "why" to the "how." The chapter presents some insight in using the marriage analogy to consider customer–supplier partnerships. Fundamentally, most firms see things almost entirely one way, with limited understanding or interest in their suppliers' views, opinions, and objectives. Almost all metrics used in state-of-the-art supply-chain management focus entirely on the supplier satisfying the customer, with nothing on what the customer needs to do and how its performance should be measured. We advocate a series of perception-based measures for both customer and supplier, since it is perceptions that matter more than "reality." Finally, the chapter presents a process we have successfully used with pairs of customers and suppliers to form partnerships and set an improvement agenda for concrete accomplishments in a reasonable time period.

- The key message is that the journey is at least as important as the destination: Achieving a pair of aces requires major changes, staying power, and the strong support of senior executives.

Chapter 7, Building the future, is concerned with the necessary changes in culture and practice that are required in order to make collaboration a way of life—rather than something that looks "wrong"—something non-competitive and non-aggressive. We see four basic components needed here: win–win, trust, strategic evolution, and misalignment. In win–win, it is absolutely imperative that both customer and supplier clearly identify the other party's goals in each major improvement effort—and that they are jointly pursued and achieved.

Trust is the fundament of collaboration, and needs to be continually nurtured. Without trust, it will be impossible to achieve anything but very low levels of collaboration that can be lost whenever a problem arises. Strategic evolution is based on the need for the partnership to have an aggressive improvement agenda—one that is shared and that has at every stage a win–win mandate. Standing still is moving backward. Finally, misalignment needs to be seen as something that will naturally occur. It is less to be avoided than to be managed, so it is important to put in place mechanisms to deal with the inevitable differences that will come up.

- Win–win partnerships must be continually nurtured, since you must be aware that they *will* go off the track occasionally: You need quick reactions, an overarching belief in the joint benefits, and good will.

Chapter 8, Changing two at a time, uses a well-known approach to change management to show how very different change management needs to be when the changes must be implemented in a pair of companies, not just one. By rigorously applying this change model (or any other well-developed change management model), you can see the need to be much more explicit about many things. Perhaps the most important of these is called "determining the desired state." What this means in our context is the need to be very clear as to the individual goals in every joint project undertaken.

A definitive win–win should be identified and be a shared objective. Moreover, it must be more than a long-run desired state. ABB might wish to increase its long-run sales to Caterpillar from $50 million to $500 million, but an immediate shared objective was a guaranteed supply of turbochargers at predictable prices, on-time deliveries, and perfect quality for Caterpillar, while ABB wished to assure this customer's loyalty, maintain a long-term relationship, and gain insights into how it might enhance the bundle of goods and services. When these have been achieved, it is possible to move on: What is next? Exploring the resultant issues includes new insights into how global account management needs to be designed: both from a supplier's point of view and the customer's. The notion of selling how the customer wants to buy takes on a new context.

- Pairs of aces must be developed jointly: Change processes have to be targeted at both supplier and customer, and they need to be synchronized—each improvement project needs to be a definite win–win.

Chapter 9, Harnessing the power of two, offers some thoughts on how you might best benefit from implementing the book's key ideas. Here we briefly provide some alternative ways you might benefit from increased collaboration with a customer or supplier. In some ways, this is an extension of Chapter 6, but now the focus is more personal: If you think the ideas in this book make sense, how might you get them implemented in your company? What might you do, and why might this be interesting and professionally rewarding?

- The key message is that you can build from sales to a few customers and/or from procurement to a few suppliers. Although there are differences, the underlying challenges, the processes, and the supporting attitude are the same.

CHAPTER 1

Picking ten partners

Most of us are familiar with the traditional Western approach to buying and selling. It is a wide-open process in which a company may juggle hundreds—or even thousands—of partners, pitting them against each other. But today, a growing number of companies are taking a radically different view. Buying at Honda, for example, is strategically based on "super suppliers"—a small number of firms with which the company works closely to develop a dominant cost advantage. In a similar fashion, selling at the engineering giant Asea Brown Boveri (ABB) is now focusing on developing special relations with key customers—increasing the total sales volume to these customers by tenfold or more.

This book's central message is that customers and suppliers can both benefit from a new form of collaboration. These radical changes are within reach, but they require serious effort and rethinking and they cannot be one-sided. The "power of two" mandates transformative changes in *both* buying and selling—changes that can be achieved only through new levels of working together.

What Honda, ABB, and other leading-edge firms understand is that close alliances with a small number of suppliers and customers can yield huge competitive advantages. Consider the following examples.

Bombardier Transportation (BT), the rail division of Bombardier Inc. ($14.8 billion annual sales as of January 31, 2007), recently created collaborative relationships with ten strategic suppliers. In each case, significant changes were required in both BT and the supplier. Included are new ways to share information, joint innovation efforts, product standardization, modularity, process simplification, and new approaches to negotiation—all supported by increased trust. The results have been very important—both for BT and for each of the suppliers.

BT started this effort by reducing its supplier base from several thousand to 500. This group was further segmented into two fundamentally different groups: those with which BT can develop collaborative relations, and those that will always be arm's length. The former group (of about 100) was further segmented into about 20 "strategic" suppliers and the rest. The ten collaborative relationships described above came from this set of 20, and the other ten are currently being prepared. In each case, the goal is to create a true partnership – what we call a "pair of aces." These 20 pairs of partners are expected to provide roughly 50 percent of the total purchasing expenditure. This implies a major increase in sales volume with each of these suppliers, significant reductions in the joint costs of doing business, and (even more importantly) critical support for new product development. If each of these partnerships can become a pair of aces, BT will have a definitive competitive advantage.

The other side of this story is playing out in leading-edge suppliers that actively help their most important customers, to:

- concentrate volumes
- reduce their supplier base
- develop regional and global procurement partnerships
- standardize their products and processes
- outsource some product development
- jointly increase supply-chain value.

Examples include:

- Cypress Semiconductor at one point partnering with Solectron (resulting in joint product development and an 18-fold increase in business for Cypress)
- Babynov, a French producer of infant food, partnering with Huhtamaki, an innovative packaging company, and Numico, an infant-food manufacturer, to jointly develop innovative products (significantly increasing sales volumes for the three partners)

- Flextronics partnering with Microsoft to support worldwide manufacture, sourcing, and logistics for the Xbox (resulting in closely matched supply with highly uncertain demand).

Subsequent chapters will examine the details of how these changes were implemented.

Each of these success stories needs to be seen not as the work of a single company. BT worked in each case with a key supplier. Cypress collaborated with Solectron. Microsoft worked together with Flextronics. These are power of two stories!

Are you an attractive customer and/or supplier? Are your most important customers and suppliers happy to work with you? Do they consider you a "partner"? Do they choose you as the one with which to share new ideas? Do they proactively encourage joint new product development efforts? Do they propose part standardization and simplification? Have you jointly moved beyond a narrow focus on unit price reduction to one of total cost of ownership?

Or do you have the opposite situation? Most US companies are still stuck in a price reduction rut. A survey of tier-one automotive suppliers consistently finds US domestic automakers rated significantly lower than their Japanese competitors in terms of working relations, with General Motors at the very bottom of the list. The gap grows every year. Recently, Yorozu America Corp., sole supplier for some key stampings, notified GM that it wished to quit working with the automaker: It could no longer tolerate GM's business practices and unilateral actions.

How about the other side? Could you definitively pick your ten most important customers—those with whom you clearly see opportunity to engage in win–win relationships? Are there one or two of these where you could jointly create a breakthrough? How are you allocating resources to these customers? Do the key account managers for these customers have different access to your engineering and other critical sources of talent? Are your senior managers actively engaged with these customers? Do you share strategies and develop scenarios for how you and this customer could create something uniquely better?

Graham Packaging went further, developing a unique working relationship with Groupe Danone over the years. Graham recently proposed building plastic blow-molding plants adjacent to Danone factories producing Actimel (a new drinkable yogurt) in order to significantly reduce time, cost, and coordination efforts between the two companies. Today, Actimel sales are in excess of 1 billion, and Graham operates seven through-the-wall plants for Danone worldwide.

Likewise, Givaudan, a flavors, fragrance, and food ingredients company, recently initiated a partnership with Unilever. The goal is to develop worldwide account management, focusing on joint value rather than just responding to price squeeze pressures.

In both cases, the benefits of collaboration are obvious. But developing the partnerships required fresh thinking and practices, with nothing obvious about the process.

Why is ten the magic number?

Developing "pairs of aces" is not a trivial job—but the objectives are not trivial either. The minimum goal for a pair of aces should be to double the productivity of the assets employed by the two companies—that is, to double the value/cost jointly created by this pair. The assets employed will be unique—as are the history, past relationship, and set of joint projects to achieve breakthrough objectives. Our experience suggests that ten major development efforts with suppliers and/or customers is an upper limit. Anyone who believes his/her company can develop more than ten winning pairs of aces in a reasonable time frame is not thinking clearly; indeed, trying to do so significantly increases chances of failure. Power of two successes require major changes in both partners and overall commitment at the top. Significant "unlearning" of past practices is often necessary.

Partnership versus partnerwhip

There is a great deal of literature and industrial hype about "partnerships." In far too many cases, this is indeed just hype—or worse—since the reality is partnership as only another negotiation trick. In some cases, the historical relationship between the firms is so bad that partnership is not even possible.

✔ General Motors has little chance of any supplier believing what it says.

An excellent partnership—a pair of aces—is not a one-way street.

Both customer and supplier need to make critical choices, to the exclusion of other choices. As in a successful marriage, there must be a long-term commitment, based on trust and mutual respect. Each partner protects the other—and this protection is not defined or mandated by legal contracts!

Figure 1.1 provides a quick review of where procurement is today, and the potential being achieved by those pushing on to the new best practice.

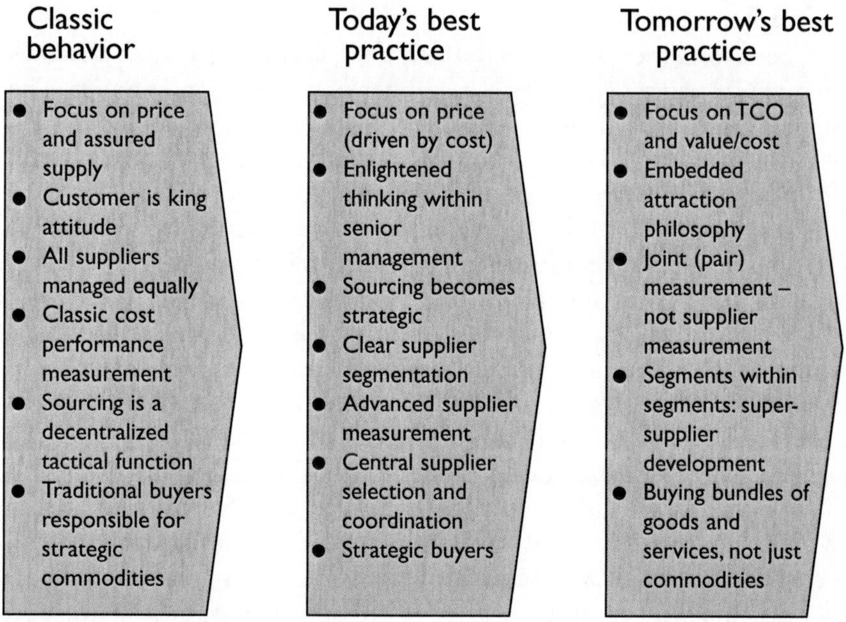

Classic behavior	Today's best practice	Tomorrow's best practice
● Focus on price and assured supply ● Customer is king attitude ● All suppliers managed equally ● Classic cost performance measurement ● Sourcing is a decentralized tactical function ● Traditional buyers responsible for strategic commodities	● Focus on price (driven by cost) ● Enlightened thinking within senior management ● Sourcing becomes strategic ● Clear supplier segmentation ● Advanced supplier measurement ● Central supplier selection and coordination ● Strategic buyers	● Focus on TCO and value/cost ● Embedded attraction philosophy ● Joint (pair) measurement – not supplier measurement ● Segments within segments: super-supplier development ● Buying bundles of goods and services, not just commodities

Figure 1.1 Procurement evolution

Procurement has been changing significantly: In recent years, the average purchasing volume as a percentage of sales has grown from something like 40 percent to over 60 percent. Currently, thinking about procurement is more enlightened: Buyers are focused on particular commodities, and volumes are concentrated. However, the key objective remains price reduction, supported by tough negotiation skills, playing off one supplier against another.

✔ Today's best practice is little more than "enlightened nonsense."

This hard-nosed approach is not necessarily bad, as long as it is not used for *all* of a company's suppliers. Figure 1.1 depicts tomorrow's best practice as a move beyond classic supplier segmentation and a single-minded focus on unit prices. Critical customer–supplier segments must be chosen and developed—a few into "pairs of aces." It is here that your firm has the chance to achieve a definitive competitive advantage: distinctly better overall value-chain performance.

The second message to be derived from Figure 1.1 is that this goes two ways: procurement by a customer is selling by a supplier. The smart supplier will also segment which customers are in which stages of Figure 1.1:How should I respond, and how might I gain from helping *some of them* move to advanced stages?

The final message in Figure 1.1 is the concept of "attraction." The customer that is most attractive will receive a greater proportion of its key suppliers' brainpower than its competitors will. That brainpower can be used to jointly create innovative solutions rather than respond to static customer specifications. Since more and more sales revenue comes from purchased items, it becomes more critical to get the best—ahead of your competitors. And you should always be on the lookout for the ideal supplier that will have flawless execution and be easier to deal with, more trust-worthy, more responsive to customer needs, more proactive, and generally regarded as "smart." Herein lies a key maxim, remembering that you should partner with only a few customers and suppliers:

✔ Never choose stupid partners!

"Smart companies" are those that clearly see the benefits in joint development—and can thereafter implement the necessary changes in culture/behavior to be the most attractive partner, and to attract the most attractive partners. Developing attraction—both as a customer and as a supplier—needs to be seen as a prerequisite to developing strategic supplier (or customer) segments. Without attraction, it will be impossible to make the big move to pair of aces development.

If your company is in the commodity business: you deserve it!

This is a strong statement, but we mean it. If your firm is selling undifferentiated commodities, life is probably pretty grim, unless you are in a cartel. Our philosophy is that no one should be in the commodity business; you must get out and stay out. This implies that you need to sell solutions and solve problems for your *key* customers. You need to work with them (which makes being attractive a prerequisite), and you must develop the strategy and supporting infrastructure to make this a reality.

IBM came to the realization some years ago that selling computers was no longer a fun business—and was one that threatened to become commoditized. The business had become cut-throat, and IBM would not survive with its high cost structures and corporate culture. So the decision was made to go into the solutions business. At the time, there was significant doubt that the company could be transformed from a bunch of box sellers to one where the approach was more like providing consulting. But IBM pulled it off.

Sony came to a similar conclusion, finding that selling consumer electronics was a very tough business. Management decided to focus on selling "content"—what comes *out* of the televisions and boom boxes—so it bought major Hollywood film and record companies. Sony had significant problems integrating the wild US filmmaking and musicmaking culture with its more staid Japanese manufacturing culture, sustaining serious losses. The company finally got everything to work together after years of turmoil. The moral is, do not underestimate the effort required to move to solutions selling.

There is an interesting flipside to selling commodities, and that is buying them. If you think of all your suppliers only as providing commodities, you may well be missing a bet. Are there one or two of these firms that could move up the value chain, more effectively taking over something that you do?

A good candidate is in logistics, where a supplier might do a much more effective job than you can. For example, Flextronics has a plant in Hungary that provides products to several major European consumer electronics companies. Flextronics also owns a third-party logistics company that delivers products directly to the European marketplace with faster response times and far lower total chain inventories. It is often possible to eliminate an inventory, delivering directly to final customers. Moreover, the overall costs of logistics are made even lower through back-hauling components to the Hungarian plant.

An even better example came up recently in our work with Bombardier Transportation. One of BT's suppliers used to sell the company a key component, as part of a larger package ("systems solution"). BT procurement switched to buying only the component, providing the other parts of the "system" on its own, and the supplier became convinced (rightly so) that it had failed to demonstrate to BT its added value—and that it must do so. Otherwise the supplier was selling commodities.

The new game

In many firms, the idea of collaborating with customers and suppliers is regarded as naïve and soft-headed, with little follow-through on pledges of working together. Doubling the payoff from pairs of aces requires that both partners definitively kill off this kind of thinking. A first requirement is that there is consensus in both companies as to how these efforts will pay off.

Where's the payoff?

What are the sources of these great payoffs? How do you double the payoff from a pair of aces? The first source of payoff is unit cost reduction. A pair of aces can perform an intensive investigation to establish a particular item's lowest possible cost; this is based on optimum production methods, best equipment, and 24/7 operations. Then it is up to the *pair* to jointly find the ways to approach this optimum—as closely as possible. Responsibility cannot be unilaterally pushed onto the supplier. Included can be joint scheduling, inventory build-ups to smooth production (with inventory costs borne by the partner best able to do so), joint investments, and many collaborative actions to eliminate transactions.

Unit cost reductions are the tip of the iceberg. More importantly, a pair can reduce non-recurring costs, reduce the numbers of procurement representatives and salespeople, reduce risks, develop product/process simplification, and implement design standardization/modularity. When switching to the numerator in value/cost, payoffs are even greater. Suppliers can greatly aid design and new product development. They also can move up the value chain, freeing the customer to provide more encompassing systems solutions. Suppliers can additionally provide more goods and services, significantly increasing the top line for the customer.

All of these payoffs are possible. The power of two is based on achieving not just one pair of aces but perhaps ten pairs—with suppliers as well as customers. This is not a short-term sales or procurement improvement effort.

The "super-supplier" pair of aces

Every customer–supplier relationship is unique, since the firms, the people that work in them, the history of the relationship, and the objectives are unique. These relationships can be improved, either incrementally or by transformation (doing the same things better or doing better things). You need to determine which few customer–supplier relationships can be developed into pairs of aces, and what will be the transformation agenda for each pair of aces: to create a *joint commitment* to transform the ways of working, determine how best to proceed, implement the ideas, observe the results, and decide what is next. Figure 1.2 illustrates the concept.

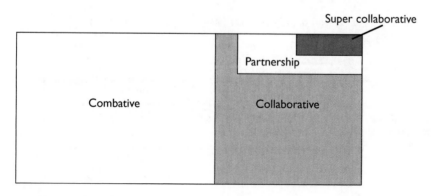

Figure 1.2 Typical mix of collaborative relationships

Figure 1.2 depicts the majority of customer–supplier relationships as "combative." For these, the focus in procurement is what we call the "rottweiler" approach: to develop the best set of negotiation experts with state-of-the-art aggressive techniques. The work is narrowly focused on one objective: lower prices through tough purchasing practices. There is no doubt that this works, and we do not suggest abandoning it. But there is an alternative—for the collaborative sector. Figure 1.2 shows less than half of the customer–supplier relationships as potentially collaborative. Within that group there is a much smaller group of strategic partnerships and an even tinier group for which super-collaborative pair of aces relations can be achieved. Figure 1.3 shows just how effective the super-collaborative concept can be. This comes from the auto industry, where Ford has held costs of incoming materials to a 7 percent increase over a six-year period, while the Consumer Price Index rose by about 11 percent. But over the same period, Honda of America reduced its similar costs by 19 percent, thus moving from a relative cost advantage over Ford of about 2 percent to one of 26 percent.

How did Honda of America manage this? Was it based on tougher negotiations? Luck? In fact, Honda's performance illustrates development of what we call "super supplier": a pair of aces where the joint actions of the customer and the supplier are vastly superior to typical arm's-length customer–supplier relations.

A benchmark comparison of programs to reduce incoming materials cost

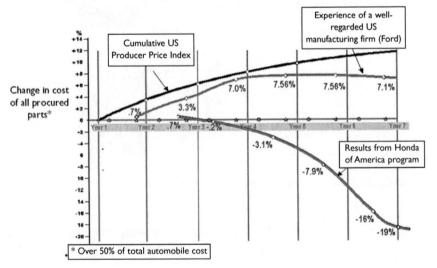

Figure 1.3 Super-supplier collaboration

Source: R. Dave Nelson, former VP Procurement, Honda of America.

In the case of Honda and its US-based super suppliers, the first partnership was with a relatively small producer of stamped sheet-metal parts. This supplier was completely committed to the pair of aces idea; did not wish to devote its existence to being in the commodity business; had a desire to excel that was widely shared in its business; and was willing to take risks, to learn, and to discard any approach in favor of a better one. Honda helped this supplier learn the industry best practices and worked with it to utilize the supplier's capacity at very high levels to "sweat the assets."

Other pairs of aces

The "super-supplier" is one pair of aces type, typically developed as explained here: A major customer (such as Honda) takes on a small or medium-sized supplier, one with the right attitude and commitment. Together, they build a relationship and set of joint working conditions with best practices and maximized capacity utilization. In the Honda example, the objective is breakthrough—a distinctively better competitive position. This cannot be done just by squeezing your suppliers. Sharper negotiation needs to be seen as necessary but insufficient. By working differently with a few pairs of aces, you can "double the return on the assets employed." In fact, doubling should be considered as modest. It is possible in some cases to increase revenues several-fold.

The second pair of aces type we have observed is the "marriage of equals." Two major firms (customer and supplier) decide, at the senior executive level, that collaboration would be much better than confrontation. Most famously, in 1987, Procter & Gamble sales VP Lou Pritchett invited Wal-Mart founder Sam Walton on a canoe trip down Arkansas's South Fork River and proposed that the two companies form a genuine partnership based on sharing information.

A third pair of aces is more like the Cypress Semiconductor–Solectron example cited in the introduction to this chapter. A large customer, having several suppliers of a similar type of products, decides to work extensively with one: Advantages of this include many-fold concentrated volumes, joint design, coordinated supply chain, enhanced bundle of goods and services, and perhaps joint selling to end customers.

Pairs of aces go beyond "improvements"

It is one thing to identify what might be a pair of aces, another to develop the necessary super-collaborative relationships; it is clearly defined working relations that deliver the payoffs. Classic sources of improvements in strategic collaboration include reducing overall inventory levels and response times, simplifying/eliminating processes such as RFQs (request for quotation), bidding, and price haggling. But breakthrough improvements can be facilitated by a third party asking the supplier "what does this customer do that costs you money?" the answers are often surprising:

- They do not pay invoices according to contractual terms, a problem that worsens near the end of their financial-reporting periods.
- They deliberately overestimate demand to be sure that we will produce enough—and to negotiate lower prices.
- They specify unnecessarily tight delivery time windows.

This works both ways. There are things the supplier does that cost the customer money (and, just maybe, your customers say these things about you):

- They ship products known to be inferior—especially when supplies are tight.
- They push inventory on the customer.
- They make promises they know they can't keep.
- They overcharge for services not explicitly in the contract.

All these can be improved, with significant benefit to joint performance. Moreover, reducing joint costs is one objective, but increasing the value can be even more important:

- How can *we* jointly bring new products to market sooner?
- Can *we* mass-customize bundles of goods and services?
- How might *we* postpone final item specification?
- Can *we* build to order instead of building to stock?
- How can *we* rapidly respond to changing market conditions?
- How can *we* reduce contractual and other bureaucratic relationships?

Super-collaborative customer–supplier relationships engage in constant benchmarking:

- benchmarking focused on the supplier operations: How to implement best-of-the-best in all processes, technologies, capacity utilization, and ways of working
- benchmarking focused on the customer: Similar push on best-of-the-best
- benchmarking focused on joint synergies: What are the absolute best ways to increase value/cost?
- benchmarking based on new relations: What are the payoffs if we increase our volume five- or tenfold?
- benchmarking on "wild ideas": Where is there an idea that could push either partner—or the pair—to make a breakthrough improvement (at least doubling or cutting in half some key metric)?

Win–win is not hitting the other person twice

Nokia uses *millions* of purchased parts per hour. To make this work effectively, the company must have an excellent supply chain. Firms such as Nokia are handling a highly perishable product; it is like buying fish in that the items need to be out of the supply chain and consumed very quickly. The value (and price) of electronic components drops at a fast rate, often as much as several percent per month. The net requirement is a supply chain that delivers huge quantities, tightly coordinated to Nokia's build schedule, with minimal inventories, and proactive price agreements that ensure the company receives the best prices its suppliers can provide. Only a limited number of firms have sufficient capacity and competencies to supply Nokia; creating the requisite supply chain mandates joint actions and a high level of coordination. Assured supply and best prices are "the ante to play" as a supplier to Nokia (and for Nokia to make it easy to play). These conditions are necessary but insufficient.

Nokia has a well-understood mandate for choosing supplier partners: There must be "shared values." Although this may sound soft, passive, overly tolerant, and unmeasurable, in fact Nokia is very serious about this concept. If the supplier and Nokia do not see the future in a consistent way, with a win–win attitude prevailing in both firms, and minimal zero-sum games, there is no point in investing the effort to create (and maintain) the collaborative mindset, the required ways of working, the joint supporting infrastructure, and the never-ending quest for improvements. In fact, "shared values" is another way of looking at joint attraction.

The concept of "shared values" implies more than usual notions of "trust." Trust is in fact a perception, and we tend to perceive that a supplier or customer is trustworthy when they act in ways we like. But the second-order issue is more profound—what gives rise to trust? The answer is what Nokia calls shared values: It and the supplier see the future in a similar way, one where what is a good outcome for one is also a good outcome for the other, and each acts in ways the other likes.

The customer leads the dance

Continuing with the importance of win–win, it is essential to make this real: As a customer, you need to become committed to the success of your supplier partners. You must help them increase their sales, their profits, and particularly their competitiveness. This clearly implies increasing the volumes through consolidation. Additionally, smart customers help supplier partners to increase and level their capacity utilization. Key suppliers should not be kept in the dark as to your plans, and certainly not suffer from uncertainty over whether they will be selected for some business. Moreover, depending upon what is being procured (e.g. size and obsolescence), it may be wise for key suppliers to sometimes produce items in advance of needs to utilize what would otherwise be idle capacity. This implies closely coordinated planning systems, as well as logistics/storage issues. The overall costs and benefits of operating in this way can be investigated and shared—with the right working relationship and attitudes. It is clearly a key element in the collaboration required for the power of two.

> ✔ Eliminate the mushroom theory of management: keep them in the dark, feed them manure, and when their heads come up, cut them off.

Smarter buying and selling

Repositioning your company with its key customers and suppliers—its *few* key customers and suppliers—requires new thinking and bold actions. For most firms there are something like ten potential pairs of aces, customers and suppliers. Experience indicates it will take several years to develop these pairs of aces. Getting things uniquely right with each pair is far more important than, for instance, implementing some computer systems and approaches that marginally improve your interactions with all customers and all suppliers. Moreover, "getting things right" is only the first step. The subsequent steps with these partners are where the major benefits are continuously achieved.

Do better things, not the same things better

You need to break out of classic approaches and thinking in both procurement and sales.

If procurement in your company is largely limited to buying routine quantities of the same goods, where the main interest is on reducing unit prices on a year-to-year basis, there is good news and bad news. The bad news is that you are missing a golden opportunity; the good news is that here is a great chance to make some major improvements. Doing so requires new ways of thinking and removing existing organizational shackles. It is much more than tinkering with existing ways of working and existing mentalities. You need entrepreneurial people, and an environment that supports them.

Hewlett-Packard (HP) procurement personnel saw that the company's internal demand for computer memory was growing exponentially, exceeding the existing supply in two to three years. The group searched the world and found a new Chinese supplier. The pricing was attractive, but the product's quality was not up to HP's requirements. Nonetheless, HP contracted for a major portion of the Chinese plant's capacity, and HP procurement located another manufacturer to whom it could *sell* this computer memory at a profit. This continued for two years, and during this time, the Chinese plant's quality improved to an acceptable level for HP, just as the company's needs were outstripping other sources of supply.

The same sort of new thinking applies equally well to your sales/marketing people. There are great opportunities to sell much more to existing customers. But you need to choose for *which* customers this makes sense. Once again, it is a choice of strategic pairs.

Skanska, the largest Scandinavian construction company, decided to form supplier partnerships with ten key suppliers, in each case on a sole source basis. One of the suppliers was Rockwool, a Swedish producer of insulation. After Skanska and Rockwool created their partnership, the two firms worked with a third-party logistics firm to coordinate deliveries to Skanska building sites from the ten suppliers. Rockwool then went back to Skanska and asked if the relationship could be expanded to encompass its Finnish parent, Partek, which makes preformed concrete products and other construction materials. This led to a major increase in sales volumes for Partek, to Skanska–Partek joint ventures in the Baltic countries and Russia, and eventually to new market segmentation for Rockwool which significantly leveraged the learning from these efforts.

Major progress does not happen by itself

Although there are some good lessons for how companies develop power of two relationships, we can offer no clear rules for how you should select the few customers and suppliers from a broader group of strategic "partners." Experience indicates that this comes from an epiphany, when senior executives in a pair of companies are able to see beyond a zero-sum model. This chapter has presented several good examples of breakout practice. In every case, an opportunity was provided for someone to take chances to break the classical mold and focus on creating a pair of aces.

In retrospect, all great improvements look obvious and easy, but this is not the case. Paradigms do not shift by themselves. Approaching a major supplier or customer with a new proposal is fraught with risk. What is needed is *joint* transformation; a combined commitment to striking out in a new direction and abandoning the current ways of working. This commitment requires senior managers in both companies to be convinced that the actions that are to be initiated are clearly in their interest.

We have developed a structured approach to developing a potential pair of aces, identifying the potential for joint work; Chapter 6 will present the details. The approach includes a two-day workshop of key personnel from both firms, which takes place after an extensive investigation process. We recently did one of these for a large company and its largest supplier. We started the workshop by presenting our analysis of the problems and opportunities, and there were some major possibilities for improvement. But the two firms' senior executives called for a timeout from our normal process—they wanted to ask themselves very critically if they wished to continue. Did they agree that this was something to which they would be willing to devote significant resources? The discussions took over an hour on each side—and the conclusion was yes. Thereafter, the process for identifying the key issues, roadblocks, and next steps went very smoothly, as did the subsequent work to make the partnership a reality, with real results for both parties. In essence, the epiphany was for each side to clearly see that collaboration would outperform negotiation.

A related issue is to take a hard look at the people involved in each of your potential pairs of aces: have you assigned the best ones? Are there some who have a reputation at the pair partner for being only a tough negotiator or not telling the truth? Can past perceptions be overcome with the existing personnel? And perhaps most importantly, are your people truly capable of adopting a win–win mentality?

> ✔ If you own a dog and you wish to own a cat, no amount of kicking the dog will accomplish your objective.

Transforming the pair requires a great deal more than good words. Specific projects require budgets and key players' dedicated time. Priorities need to be established and periodic progress assessments need to be made. Sliding back to old ways is an ever-present danger, and complacency must be avoided: Good enough is never good enough! A fundamental requirement is for some form of ombudsman activity to be established for each pair, to escalate the inevitable squabbles to a level where they can be worked out before becoming serious. In pair of aces partnerships, you find the long-term development of cooperative working relationships, a willingness to jointly study opportunities—without formal agreements—and unwritten rules of behavior.

HP provides still another example. HP and Canon have worked together for many years, and the relationship has progressed to one of shared values, mutual trust, and a joint vision of the future and how they can work together. One result is an unwritten rule at HP—*if you screw up the Canon relationship, you will get fired.*

So what?

If price reduction is the only tool in your procurement bag, you are headed for trouble. Similarly, if the sole response to your customers' price pressures is reduction at the expense of your margins, you have an equally bleak future. If your company has not recently rethought its relationship with its ten most important customers and suppliers, you are missing a good bet for enhancing your competitive position. This can deliver big bang for the buck, but the efforts must not be underestimated. Transforming these relationships requires collaboration—pairs of aces. Do not even try to do the same thing for a large number of suppliers; the effort will surely fail. Similarly, there are only a few customers that will be responsive to major collaboration. The key pairs must be ones in which mutual trust is possible.

Unlearning and major organizational changes will be needed (people, approach, and senior-management support/belief). The risks of falling back to old behaviors (e.g. classic buying/selling) are ever-present. You need to learn—from procurement to sales, and vice versa. Continually compare processes, progress, and learning points. Sales needs to understand the new game needed in procurement, and procurement needs to understand that in sales. Seeing these as two sides of the same coin is a key ingredient in the power of two.

Finally, achieving these benefits is a major leadership challenge. Senior managers will need to prioritize customer–supplier pairs, develop key contacts, select and motivate the right people internally, drive the change agenda, assess progress, and continually improve the focus. None of this is easy, but it is the best game in town.

Picking ten partners is a strategic choice—a mandate—that focuses your company's attention on the few breakout opportunities available. In the next chapter, we describe four stages of collaboration to achieve this mandate.

CHAPTER 2

Mastering the four stages of collaboration

Chapter 1 presented the fundamental ideas of the power of two, some · examples, and the need for selection/development of particular customer–supplier partnerships. In all of this, there is an overriding need for joint efforts: It takes two to tango. But more importantly, there are ever-increasing payoffs to be derived from these collaborative relationships. The power of two has the overriding goal that collaboration should exponentially increase competitive advantage: 2 squared, then 2 cubed, etc.

Collaboration was shown in Figure 1.2 as comprising less than half of all relationships with suppliers, and within this set, there are still smaller subsets (leading to the elusive pairs of aces). The power of two will need to be developed one customer–supplier pair at a time, recognizing the unique nature of each firm and each set of historical relationships. The joint work is heavy, and experience shows something like ten to be the upper limit at any one time.

The goal of Chapter 2 is to clarify the meaning of customer–supplier collaboration, to examine what is implied for both buyer and seller, and to clearly indicate the power of two differences in four stages of collaboration: in the collaborative work, in the attitudes required, and in the results that should be expected. Chapter 2 also explores governance processes needed to support collaborative efforts—at any stage—and, more importantly, to shift one collaborative stage to the next. None of this is easy, many natural barriers exist, and senior managerial commitment—by both companies—is required to create the win–win results (to generate the power of two).

Collaboration does not just happen and always requires trust. Moreover, when (not if) the trust is broken, repair efforts need to be made as soon as possible. The usual cause for a breach in trust is one person making a decision that seems to be good for his or her firm, but that comes at the expense of the other firm. The implication is that collaboration and trust need to be based on going beyond zero-sum thinking and actions. But saying this is so does not make it happen.

> It is important that each firm have a policy to resist zero-sum actions with a partner. Moreover, it is equally important that each partner does not perceive that such actions are taken by the other party. We have witnessed many wild stories about specific customer or supplier behaviors that prove to be far from accurate. We have also seen cases in which one person or group in a company has a completely different opinion from another. Collaboration and trust require that perceptions be managed.

Let us now develop the four stages or levels of collaboration. Fundamentally, these need to be seen as sequential efforts, each setting up the necessary conditions for the subsequent level, but recognizing that each level requires new focus, new joint work, and a new cast of characters. Each stage generates its own power of two payoffs, and each successive stage carries the work and benefits to new levels.

Figure 2.1 depicts the four stages of collaboration, along with the key players who need to be active in each stage. In stage 1—flawless execution—we see the two firms necessarily working jointly to be sure that the right products are delivered at the right time, with the right cost. This involves operational people in both companies doing whatever is necessary. Note that the demarcation between the supplier and customer—at all four stages—is not clear. Problems need to be solved, by those best able to do so, with minimum parochialism. At the second stage—total cost of ownership—the cast of characters now includes the accountants, plus those who will redesign the joint company systems and processes. At the third level—value/cost—we see the inclusion of design and procurement

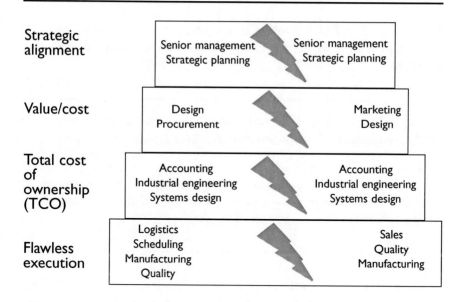

Figure 2.1 The four stages of collaboration

people at the supplier, and design and marketing people at the customer. The joint goal is to enhance the customer's offerings in its marketplace, through new design, smarter buying, and faster response. Finally, at the fourth stage—strategic alignment—we need the senior managers in both companies to interact, and their subsequent strategic planning to reflect their resulting joint wishes.

Stage 1: flawless execution

In several chapters, we state that flawless execution is "the ante to play," meaning that if the basics (delivery times, quality, and cost) are not being achieved, there is little chance to develop collaborative relationships. But there is a fundamental difference between compliance and collaboration. The former exists in any supply chain relationship: A customer specifies delivery times and specific quality attributes, prices are determined through negotiation and contractual obligation, and measurements focus exclusively on vendor performance. In collaboration, all of these need to be seen as subject to *joint* determination, where the objective is overall optimization, with total joint cost as one key component.

Moreover, in collaboration it is essential to not assume that any execution problems are the fault of the supplier rather than the customer.

Many companies agree on service-level objectives, such as the percentage of on-time deliveries. But in one case, we saw a supplier with 98 percent on-time deliveries and an unhappy customer – the other 2 percent caused major problems. The same customer had another supplier with much lower on-time delivery performance but a close collaboration on planning (which was somewhat volatile for the customer), so that the customer very rarely experienced shortages from this supplier.

There is a vast literature dealing with flawless execution, coming from industrial engineering roots and now including lean manufacturing thinking and a wide range of quality improvement ideas. These are beyond our present scope. Here we focus on the collaborative efforts needed to apply these execution principles—jointly.

A just-in-time example

Automobile manufacturers typically purchase car seats from a specialized seat-manufacturing company such as Johnson Controls or Lear, manufactured and delivered on a just-in-time (JIT) basis. That is, a firm such as Volkswagen provides Johnson Controls with its exact build sequence for something like 48 hours in the future. Johnson Controls does not build any car seats to inventory; they are completely assembled in the same order as the build schedule within the 48-hour time frame and delivered, in sequence, directly to the VW assembly line. That is, there are no car seats in inventory at either Johnson Controls or VW; there is no VW work involved in selecting/picking car seats from inventory or moving car seats from some central location to the proper place on the assembly line; there are no "orders" for seats, and no "invoices" for deliveries. VW and Johnson Controls can rest assured that if the car was assembled, it had a seat; therefore this seat needs to be paid for. The savings in indirect costs by both VW and Johnson Controls are significant. Moreover, the minimal amount of handling involved reduces the opportunities for damage.

✔ This process needs to be recognized for what it is: a high-wire act.

Making this JIT system work requires flawless execution on the part of both companies. Johnson Controls must be able to build and deliver in the 48-hour time slot, and the quality must be perfect. There is no other seat available if one is defective. They must be delivered in the exact sequence: The assembly team reaches for the next seat that is green—and here comes a green car! VW cannot change the sequence, or the green seat may end up in a red car. And it works both ways, since for the same reason, a defective car cannot be removed from the line.

This example clearly illustrates the potential productivity gains in collaborative efforts. It also shows that flawless execution is the job of both customer and supplier. But collaboration implies even more: With production so closely tied together, Johnson Controls and VW need to continually look for ways to enhance their productivity. What might Johnson Controls do additionally that would reduce downstream work at VW?

Collaboration driven by the customer

The flipside of Johnson Controls doing work to enhance VW operations is an automotive company working on what it might do to make life easier for its supplier. Would it help Johnson Controls if the build schedule were frozen for 60 hours instead of 48?

Over the years, we have had many discussions with automotive-part suppliers, with one consistent conclusion: Toyota is the best customer. Why? It makes it easy to achieve flawless execution, it does not assume that problems are only the fault of the supplier, it is willing to send in experts to help solve problems, and it will make changes on its side to make execution more straightforward. Toyota provides suppliers with more information, it makes fewer changes, it has far fewer crises, and its designs work with far fewer modifications.

✔ Toyota has moved from a "compliance" mode to one of collaboration.

The level of collaboration is, of course, different from supplier to supplier, but new suppliers to Toyota are usually surprised by the

openness and help provided to them. Chapter 1 noted that asking
suppliers what the customer does that costs them money always
yields good responses—responses that the customer should see as
"gold nuggets." More fundamentally, the two firms must regard all
problems as *our* joint opportunities, not as items to add to the other
company's to-do list.

The JIT example illustrates still one more issue in flawless execution: The definition of what precisely it is can and should change
over time. This is particularly so when customers and suppliers
rethink their relative roles in the value chain. Many times, the
supplier can move up the value chain, taking over work that was
traditionally done by the customer, freeing the customer to do the
same for *its* customers. It is continually winning the orders from
these customers that really matters.

An early example was Procter & Gamble providing Wal-Mart
warehouses with products sequenced for subsequent delivery to
stores. Later providing products that included price markings
enhanced this. But today, by including bar codes and RFID technology, it is possible for Wal-Mart to know the location and age of
every item in its supply chain.

Finally, a few words of caution. Flawless execution costs money.
Design engineers need to improve quality. Process engineers need to
enhance manufacturing methods. Systems engineers need to design
and implement new computer systems. Suppliers need to visit
customers, and vice versa. Networking needs to be maintained—
and enhanced as individuals move on to new positions. Benchmarking and understanding what constitutes best state-of-the-art
practices takes time and effort. It is far too easy to degrade these
practices through some misguided cost reduction efforts. All of them
are far too important to be left for when someone has the time. But
none should be a waste of time: They represent some of the best
ways to enhance your firm's productivity and competitive position.
If they are explicitly focused on particular customer–supplier pairs,
it will be easier to match the costs with the benefits.

Stage 2: total cost of ownership

With flawless execution seen as an issue of collaboration, not
compliance, and results matching expectations, it is possible to
move on to stage 2, total cost of ownership (TCO). In some ways,

this is a natural evolution from stage 1, but it is better to see it as a shift—a new emphasis—with new goals and some new ways to achieve them. In essence, stage 2 needs to be seen as moving from 2 squared to 2 cubed. This implies new thinking, new objectives, and further unlearning of classic ideas. What does not change, however, is the idea of joint efforts and trust—in fact, these must be significantly enhanced.

There is, again, significant literature on TCO concepts which we do not wish to review here. Our focus is on TCO as providing a new focus for collaboration: one in which all costs, direct and indirect— in both customer and supplier—are seen as targets for elimination or significant improvement. The underlying assumption is that these can be improved only jointly, and that it is often one firm's new approaches that take cost out of the other. For example, the inherent speed in JIT allows standard thinking for inventory transactions to be discarded. There are so few completed seats at Johnson Controls or at VW that neither firm needs to worry about them. Whatever their number, the volume is close to constant (45 minutes of stock is less than 5 percent of one day's volume).

Transparency

The basic idea in TCO is to make all costs visible so that they can be reduced or eliminated. Experience shows that this—however laudable as an objective—can be quite difficult. The primary problem is a lack of trust and experience, originating from the combative history of customer–supplier relationships. That is, all suppliers have experience with one or more customers asking for "open books." In practice this usually turns out to be nothing more than another price negotiation tactic. In order to actually achieve cost transparency, it is probably essential to have gone through something like stage 1, where all problems become seen as "joint," where resources are applied as required and a critical level of trust has been established.

There is much more to TCO than open books, essentially accounting documents designed for classic product costing. In fact, what is needed for TCO is much more comprehensive. In the JIT example, where would any standard accounting system report the benefits of speed improvement, elimination of orders/invoices, coordinated processes, or damage reduction? If TCO starts with classic cost

accounting, then there is a natural tendency to fall back to price negotiation. This should be avoided. The product costs shown in a standard cost accounting system will often be dominated by material
costs, and the others may be just as difficult to reduce.

✔ The focus needs to be on *all* costs—ones that can be
   eliminated. The prices are the passengers, not the drivers.

A good example comes from the Honda super-supplier story in Chapter 1. The key cost to be eliminated by the supplier was that of excess
capacity: What could be the result if the supplier ran at high capacity
on a 24/7 basis? How much is sweating the assets worth? Is it necessary to estimate this cost saving to three decimal places? Hardly. The
savings are large, both firms can wait to see what the actual savings
become, and thereafter a reasonable division can be made (win–
win, power of two). In fact, the real goal is for key people in both
companies to see the power and look for what is next.

In a well-run TCO study, the focus should jointly be on whatever
costs in either company might be eliminated or sharply reduced, and
what joint actions would be necessary to achieve this result. This
implies auditing of processes, and not just at the supplier firm. They
need to be compared to the best in class. The breakthrough for
Toyota's JIT manufacturing system came from studying replenishment in a supermarket!

The expectation is that the pair (two firms) changing the ways in
which they jointly operate can most effectively reduce total costs. If
the cost reduction is to be achieved by making changes in only one
firm, a reasonable assumption is that such reductions have already
been largely achieved.

Systems integration

A key issue in TCO concerns whether a supplier should provide
the customer with components or an integrated system. Another
way of looking at the issue is whether the resulting system is more
than the sum of its parts. Making this decision requires some critical analysis of "costs," many which will not reside in standard
systems. For example, if the customer buys a system instead of all
the components of the system, what is the impact on the indirect
costs of procurement and associated transaction costs? What are

the true costs of assembly in both situations? Who is more techni-
cally qualified to not only assemble but enhance the design? Who
should have the downstream responsibility for failure and maintenance? Are there key issues in terms of intellectual property or
core competence that accompany this decision? Finally, decisions
like this need to be based on future expectations. Is buying integrated systems more in line with an evolving outsourcing strategy
for the customer?

Life cycle costing

TCO ideas can also be applied to a product over its life cycle. This
is an issue for Bombardier Transport (BT) and the railroad cars it
makes. A key question is whether BT can make the cars with more
expensive components that would permit longer times between
maintenance/replacements. The answer is a clear yes, but without
trust and shared understanding, it is very difficult for BT to sell
these ideas to most of its customers.

Life cycle costing is an appealing concept, which gains in appeal
as you apply it to more stages in the value chain. It does indeed
make more sense to consider the total cost, from a hole in the
ground to final disposal of the product. Unfortunately, this turns out
to be impractical: It is hard enough to get two firms to discuss joint
total costs; three or more is usually impossible.

We once made a detailed study of a supply chain that included a
steel manufacturer making tin plate, a can company making cans, a
paint company filling the cans, and a retailer selling the paint. Each
firm was losing money, and each was trying to reduce costs by pushing problems onto the others (e.g. you hold the inventory, not me).
But our study indicated that the overall chain held 40 weeks of
inventory! Moreover, the final customers seemed interested in innovation (new colors) and were impressed by better looking cans. But
the system was saddled with a 40-week lead time, as well as a can
manufacturer who saw printed labels as a good cost reduction.

Our advice is to take on only what you and a partner (supplier or
customer) can control, which limits your search for cost improvements
to a pair of companies and focuses attention on what it is possible to
implement. Your search should include visits to each other's facilities,
examination of how the customer uses the supplier's products, the indirect costs, capacity utilizations in both firms, comparisons with other

customers and suppliers, benchmarking against best in class, and generation of wild ideas. (A Johnson & Johnson team interested in setup time reduction observed a Formula 1 racing team change a set of tires.) The search can also include financial benchmarking of other companies for indirect costs such as sales expenses, general/administrative, and logistics. Sometimes, the differences will turn out to be due to different accounting conventions, but not always. Complexity costs money, and it will be shown somewhere.

Stage 3: value/cost

The third stage in the power of two collaborative efforts is to shift definitively away from cost as the sole determinant of competitive advantage. The new idea is to work with the ratio of value to cost, where the numerator is perhaps even more important than the denominator. This shift leads immediately to joint product design. A natural extension of buying integrated systems is to enfranchise the supplier to design these systems. But an even better solution is some form of joint design incorporating the supplier's design capabilities with the customer's knowledge of the product in use. Moreover, the pair of two firms can jointly determine overall best component sourcing approaches, particularly in the use of common parts, and standardization efforts.

A new cast of characters

When collaborative efforts enter stage 3, the main actors need to be significantly augmented. It is important to retain those in both firms who have been instrumental in developing the right attitudes that foster collaboration and smooth the waters as need be. But now there are new possibilities opening that require additional inputs. Product designers on both sides will need to develop networking as well as shared understanding about intellectual property and issues of confidentiality/exclusivity.

Nokia works with many suppliers in the development of new products. For example, Nokia and Texas Instruments (TI) have often worked on the joint properties needed in a new microchip, which thereafter TI has developed. The long-run expectation is that TI will sell this chip to Nokia's competitors—after an agreed-upon time period during which Nokia will be able to use it in Nokia phones exclusively.

✔ There is no way that your firm has all the smartest people working for it.

Your suppliers have many ideas, and if you can develop the pairs that incorporate key supplier knowledge into your products, you will gain a competitive advantage. Doing so mandates a win–win approach in which those key suppliers view your firm as first choice for where to work jointly.

Managers at the baby food company Numico calculated the percentage of sales in R&D for their key suppliers; this they multiplied by their net sales to those suppliers, to determine how much Numico was contributing to the suppliers' R&D. Then they pointedly asked what they were receiving for their "investments."

The collaborative efforts in stage 3 require greater managerial inputs than those of the prior stages, because the impact is across more of the organization. Marketing needs to determine which products and features would be market winners, design engineering must work in trustful ways with selected suppliers, supply chains need to be coordinated, new product introduction and logistics must reflect the resultant set of decisions, and expectations need to be managed (we turn to governance in a later section).

Long-run R&D collaboration

A collaborative value/cost approach implies a long-run horizon for the customer–supplier pair. This means that it should be possible to jointly develop long-term planning for the customer products of the future, and how the supplier might best help the customer achieve these goals. An example is ABB and Caterpillar, and their joint developments for diesel engines. ABB, as a premier manufacturer of turbochargers, can help Caterpillar achieve increased engine performance—doing so with reduced pollution. But ABB also has core technical competencies in combustion, sensing, and emissions control. All of these are of potential value to Caterpillar in its development of next-generation diesel engines. The task before this pair of firms is how to find the best mode of collaboration to develop the true win–win.

Top-line growth

One major source of competitive advantage in stage 3 is greater use of suppliers to increase overall sales. Resources such as the number of engineers, R&D laboratory, manufacturing facilities, and logistics limit the ability of any company to design, manufacture, and sell. Like other firms, Hewlett-Packard has recognized the value in its brand name and increasingly works with supplier companies to develop product offerings that require limited resource inputs from HP. Making this a reality mandates new competences in procurement, the alignment/networking of in-house engineering with key suppliers, supply chain integration, and new quality procedures. It is worth noting that in recent years, several large firms such as Mattel have seriously underestimated the need for quality control in China. The key learning point here is, again, that collaboration focused on value/cost enhancement requires new work and new efforts; it also requires new attention to achieving and maintaining flawless execution.

A related question is whether stage 3 is more than simply outsourcing manufacturing, or if the prior two stages need to be implemented first.

✔ The key distinction comes back to compliance versus collaboration.

When outsourcing is based solely on specifications, the customer has to assume that the supplier will find the minimum cost way to meet these specifications. In fact, the entire approach encourages the supplier to do so. In some cases, this is in fact a good approach. But when the issue is value/cost improvement, the sole focus should not be on the denominator. Moreover, if the resultant products damage the customer's brand name, a serious error has been made.

It is interesting to contrast the recent experience with Chinese toy manufacturers and the use of contract manufacturing companies by food companies such as Nestlé. Because large food manufacturers typically lack facilities to make items in small batches, they generally introduce new products though having them made by contract manufacturers. If a new product is a success, then major investments are made to set up dedicated facilities. But since the cost of an error (product recall) is so high in the food industry, the quality controls over all facilities are uniformly high. Firms such as Nestlé clearly understand the risks with particular materials and processes. Nestlé would never leave key risks unattended, regardless of who owns the manufacturing facility.

Stage 4: strategic alignment

The final stage in power of two collaboration is strategic alignment. This stage requires an even greater commitment at senior management level, but it also requires structured means to diffuse the work throughout the organizations on both sides. Let us take an evolutionary view on how two firms can end up at stage 4.

Figure 2.2 depicts the four stages as a funnel. The number of customer–supplier partnerships that pass though each stage is progressively less. Each stage is built on success in the prior stages.

Moving from stage 1 to stage 4

Collaboration typically starts with a project, a business unit, or some other organizational unit in one firm connecting with another in a customer or supplier firm. Using our four-stage approach,

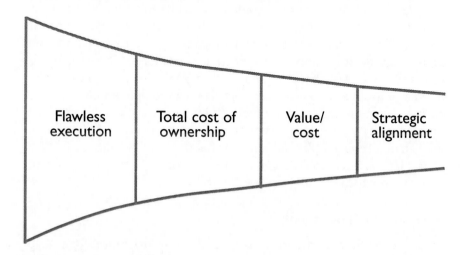

Figure 2.2 Progressive collaboration stages

perhaps there is a straightforward problem of execution, such as from poor communication of schedule dates between the firms. Assuming this was solved through collaboration rather than forced compliance, the result might be shared good feelings on the parts of those who jointly solved the problem. Perhaps other issues associated with flawless execution also come up, and these too are solved through collaborative work.

A next step might be to focus on total cost of ownership, with the same individuals playing the major role, but now adding others to support analysis of costs, development of alternative solutions, and implementation of new systems/processes. An example might be elimination of one inventory at the customer firm, with transparency of the same inventory at the supplier firm being available to the customer, and joint efforts to plan replenishments and disbursements. Clearly, implementing this kind of change would require collaborative efforts among a wider set of people than those to solve classic execution problems.

When we move to stage 3, value/cost, the sales and marketing folks need to come in, as do design engineers on both sides. But the particular people will be selected based on the exact enhancements anticipated. If, for example, the supplier will make a new product with the customer's brand name, the marketing people associated with this product line will be involved, as will the supply chain that moves this kind of product out to its customers.

Stage 4 is a much more encompassing collaboration between the customer and the supplier. One way to move to this level would be for the supplier to adopt a strategy of significant organic growth, based on selling significantly more to its existing client base. This strategy is precisely what ABB has adopted, with a goal of increasing its sales tenfold or more to selected customers. This cannot happen through the existing business channels, no matter how well they collaborate. The sales of ABB to Caterpillar were at some point just over $50 million, with an objective of $500 million plus. But the existing sales were heavily in turbochargers to the large-engine division of Caterpillar—not an easy site in which to ramp up sales tenfold.

A new level of networking

To achieve the growth objective, ABB must do more than help Caterpillar with design of its next generation of diesel engines. ABB now needs to penetrate other divisions and business units of Caterpillar. To do so, it needs to leverage existing successful collaborative efforts and jointly develop a win–win approach that goes beyond the present connections. One way to view this is for ABB personnel to identify the "white spaces" inside Caterpillar: Those places where ABB products and technology could be applied. A similar challenge exists for Caterpillar: It needs to carefully analyze the capabilities and technical competencies of ABB and develop some sort of roadmap for which divisions and business units can best leverage these supplier assets.

An example is a new factory being designed by Caterpillar. How much of the equipment for this factory (robots, electrical, etc.) might ABB provide? And why would Caterpillar wish to buy these goods from ABB instead of on the open market? Answers to these questions are key to stage 4 collaboration. ABB will put their best resources into working with Caterpillar on this plant with the expectation that the new facility will be the best, the most productive, and on-stream/ramped up to capacity faster than with any other option.

✔ This leads to the hard part: how to make it happen—on both sides.

The pair of firms needs to recognize that the good support and networking that presently exists between ABB and Caterpillar is in only one small pocket of the potential business. There is a significant challenge for ABB to develop the many sets of collaborative relationships needed for a key customer such as Caterpillar. But there is an equal set of challenges on the customer side. Someone at a very senior level needs to decide *which* suppliers are the ones— remember our rule of ten! The clear win–win needs to be articulated, developed, communicated, and assessed. There will be significant resistance to making the necessary changes, in both the customer and the supplier firms.

In fact, there will be many who see this kind of collaborative relationship as unworthy of the trouble. They are not totally wrong. Strategy is choice, and the choices made here are critical to the long-run success of both firms which will make the necessary investments in time and networking development to achieve the necessary results.

Governance

Collaboration can indeed make major payoffs to those who get it right. We have already cautioned that it isn't easy. We can add that it needs guidance. Collaboration may be possible to achieve without a plan or some sort of governance, but it is nearly impossible to sustain without one. We have witnessed good collaborative efforts that depended too much on the goodwill and informal support of particular individuals. Governance needs to be seen as an overriding process—one that requires ownership by some sort of joint steering committee that assesses progress, eliminates roadblocks, sets priorities, and facilitates improvements.

Fitting governance to the task

In early stages of collaboration, when the shift has been essentially one of moving from compliance, the primary need is to develop a sense of shared problems: These are *ours*, not *yours* or *mine*. In practice, when attacking issues in flawless execution, what seems to work is a steering group that meets on a regular schedule—perhaps quarterly—and that assigns sets of tasks to particular individuals to complete. They in turn are expected to come to the steering group meeting and report progress.

A further development we have found useful is a quarterly online survey to many people in both firms which asks their perceptions of execution, working relationships, trust, and progress. These take little time to fill out and are based on a 1-to-7 point scale of agreement with the idea. By keeping a time series of these responses, the collaborative relationship is less likely to find itself unexpectedly in trouble.

One of the major challenges in collaboration is measurement.

> ✔ It is better to measure the right things approximately than the wrong ones exactly.

Perceptions are what really matter in collaboration, so let these be a key part of how you evaluate the results. In the end, it is the opinions of individuals that matter, and you need continually to be on the lookout for bad stories, as well as for complacency. In order to truly achieve the power of two, it is critical for the personnel in both customer and supplier to remain passionate and committed to enhancing the relationship.

There is a natural evolution in the work of the steering commit-tee. It typically starts with whatever execution problems exist, assigning people from both firms to fix them—quickly. The prob-lems tend to escalate into opportunities, along the lines of the shift from stage 1 to stage 2. However, a definitive shift does make sense, since thereafter you will be looking for opportunities that will be less obvious. One set that we have seen several times is a definitive focus on "non-recurring costs." These include issues such as how much effort is being put into requests for quotation, detailed pricing, and overly complex contractual obligations.

Life cycle costing ideas are useful in some situations, but they usually need to be preceded by contracts that make one party responsible for the product over its useful life cycle. Several times, we have witnessed situations where the companies involved in this process have been quite surprised at the size of the downstream cost requirements.

When collaboration moves away from the immediate problems of flawless execution, it becomes increasingly difficult to isolate the costs, the benefits, and to whom those benefits flow. Experience indicates that a long-run view on this is important, realizing that the overriding goal has to be for the customer to be most effective in its marketplace. Without this, there are no real benefits to share. Infus-ing this concept throughout a pair of organizations takes consider-able effort, and it must be continually supported by the actions and words of senior managers.

The limit of "ten"

Governance issues obviously grow in importance as you move from stage 1 to stage 4. In fact, the number of stage 4 relationships that any firm can support is severely limited. There is only so much managerial attention and only so much detailed collabora-tion that can be supported. Hewlett-Packard talks about its special relationship with Canon, but it does not say the same thing about other firms. Sure, there are some that it works with intensively, but strategic alignment sets the bar very high.

The ombudsman

Finally, governance issues need to have someone to solve prob-lems. Do not assume they will not occur—they will. What is important is that there is a process with key individuals on both sides to find the ways to resolve any problem—turn it into an opportunity, and assign a joint group to solve it! Appointing one person in each company as ombudsman puts these two individuals in a special role on the steering committee. Rather than a primary concern with the "what," the ombudsmen are concerned with the "how." They focus on continually strengthening the "glue" that holds the pair together, and how to rapidly solve the inevitable clashes that will occur—solve minor problems before they become major problems.

All the stages

Collaborative relationships can indeed evolve from stage 1 to stage 4. But stage 1 problems can and will come up from time to time. As the relationship grows to cover more and more of the business units and divisions, there will be many challenges and opportunities. One thought here is to continually keep a record of the things that have been achieved. It will be good reading whenever someone doubts the validity of the collaboration.

So what?

The power of two is based on the principle of collaboration. Sometimes, two firms can develop a win–win approach at a senior managerial level and thereafter develop a winning combination— a pair of aces. This pair starts out to solve all execution problems collaboratively, not through rules and coerced compliance. The initial results are typically a good working relationship and satisfaction on both sides. Moving on to the second stage, where all costs in both firms are examined, usually leads to costs that are not shown in any financial system but are nonetheless real. Reducing them requires new levels of trust and collaboration. Moving on to joint value creation and finally to strategic alignment requires much greater efforts, but the rewards are equally significant (win–win). In all of this, there is a need for some governance processes. Collaboration will not occur by itself, and there are many places where it can go off the rails.

The key message in this chapter is that collaboration needs to be mastered, and that recognizing four distinct stages can provide a roadmap to achieving best practice. In Chapter 3, we want to apply these collaborative ideas in procurement: How can you pick the best ten potential suppliers and develop them into pairs of aces? Both customer and supplier will need to continually believe that each new initiative is a win–win.

CHAPTER 3

Restructuring procurement

In March 2007, Airbus announced a major overhaul to its operations. Its objective is to cut annual costs by €2 billion and generate cumulative savings of €5 billion by 2010. The lion's share of the cost savings are to come from reducing headcount by 10,000; outsourcing 50 percent of the airframe structure (double the existing level); developing ten tier-one risk-sharing partners, and gaining 31 percent of the total savings from "smart buying." Airbus also sees itself becoming much more of a systems integrator than a fabricator.

This is a tremendous challenge, implying a massive change agenda, overcoming huge barriers (the unions are calling for Europe-wide coordinated strike action as this is being written). Most importantly for our purposes, making this a reality requires major rethinking in the approaches to procurement and to the support of these new approaches by the other parts of the company. Can Airbus pull it off? Time will tell.

Achieving this kind of transformation for Airbus—and for you—requires the following imperatives:

- A purely combative approach to procurement will not work. Airbus must *truly* develop the ten tier-one risk-sharing partners.
- The supply base for Airbus (and for you) must be segmented into that part for which even stronger combative approaches

are right and that which supports the collaborative approach.
- Many of the existing purchasing personnel will need to greatly change their ways—or be replaced. Collaboration is a very different game.
- Airbus (and you) will need to become the most attractive customer to the most important suppliers.
- Pairs of aces must be developed. This is the only way to achieve the overall objectives.
- Winning the game mandates joint changes (power of two) in ways to manage buying (by you) and selling (by your key suppliers).

Leveraging the collaborative segment

Airbus is saying the right things. The best way for this manufacturer to become truly competitive is to significantly move up the value chain: outsource much of manufacturing; concentrate on design, new product development, and systems integration; and work closely with a small number of key suppliers. All of this implies developing pairs of aces, substituting collaborative relations for the classic combative relations. Airbus's choice of the number ten for risk-sharing partners does not surprise us. The magic *ten* keeps coming up in many circumstances. Although not some absolute rule, it does create a boundary—an appropriate order of magnitude that is possible. Focusing on only ten suppliers concentrates attention on the huge scope of the task with each of them. More importantly, limiting the number to ten creates high expectations. The objective in each case is not incremental improvement, and it is the ten pairs of aces that will transform procurement to create a competitive advantage, and do so with significant payoffs for both players.

Saying so doesn't make it so

Massive changes in procurement such as those envisioned for Airbus need a consistent strategy and ways of thinking about the complex set of issues. But the right objectives are the smallest part of the process. Similarly, locating and developing the ten risk-sharing partners is only the start of the game. We often find that a marriage analogy is used for customer–supplier partnerships:*

✔ Obtaining a contract for a supply chain partnership is about as useful as a marriage license for achieving a happy married life.

It is quite surprising how often we encounter a firm that makes statements about supplier partnership which are really just nonsense. Peugeot's website recently bore the title: "Modernise our purchasing process to optimize our collaboration." This was followed by a statement about how this was to work: "Through reverse e-auctions we bring transparency to our relationships."

E-auctions might even be a good idea—especially for routine items such as copy paper. But they need to be recognized for what they are: A more efficient combative approach that does not fit with developing major payoffs through collaboration.

For serious purchased items, especially those where suppliers need to make investments in capital that are uniquely tied to these items, the collaborative model becomes critical. This is clearly the case for the major airframe components at Airbus. The supplier and customer must jointly determine how to maximize the capacity utilization of those capital assets, and how to use them most efficiently. The goal needs to be asset management by the collaborating pair of companies, not one gaining at the expense of the other. This is clearly the route to the significant competitive advantage developed by Honda that we saw in Chapter 1 (the super supplier).

Are you helping your key suppliers to better utilize their capacity? Do you jointly make plans and then execute them on your end as promised? Are you so focused on inventory metrics inside your organization that you are sub-optimizing inventory in the supply chain? Are you pushing costs onto your suppliers that you could more easily manage? Do you stretch out payment terms to your suppliers when in fact your cost of capital is lower?

---

* We realize that what we call marriage is perhaps a bit more like polygamy, and that "divorce" is clearly a possibility. In fact, supply chain partnerships require a long-term commitment, but are sometimes dissolved—usually when one partner decides that collaboration is not in its best interest. This most often occurs when there is a change in senior management.

Win–win means winning together

Collaboration starts with the belief that there are much greater benefits to be obtained through working jointly than through playing zero-sum games. It is important to move beyond unit price to the total set of costs that are born in a customer–supplier pair, finding the ways to minimize the total through joint actions, linked infrastructure, and shared goals. But making win–win a reality requires definitive payoffs that will accrue to each party, a process to measure these payoffs, and mutual trust to ensure that they will in fact result.

A large telecom company found that the total inventory in its supply chain with a major customer was more than 200 days. But with another customer, the corresponding inventory was less than ten days. The telecom firm designed a new way for orders to flow from the first customer; it also proposed closing the local warehouse in the country and fulfilling orders from a regional warehouse. The net result was expected to reduce the total pipeline inventory to something on the order of 75 days—a major saving. The amazing thing about this example, though, is that the telecom company called this effort a "win–win program" when in fact the customer perceived no benefit from it. The telecom firm was much surprised when the major customer resisted the improvements, pointing out that it wanted more inventory in the pipeline in order to respond to unexpected demand. As a consultant, one of us pointed out the problem to the telecom company, suggesting that since it would be reducing inventory by 125 days—and cash-to-cash cycle by a similar amount—why not give the customer the incentive of stretching out accounts payable terms by something like 30 days? The accountants soundly rejected this idea, and the program never achieved its desired objectives.

Unilateral actions and unilateral demands for customers or suppliers to change their ways of working are rarely successful—unless there is a clear-cut payoff for the other party. Experience indicates that people are so focused on the payoffs for their own company that they do not pay adequate attention to making win–win a reality. Moreover, zero-sum thinking is so ingrained that the idea of the other person getting any payoff is often anathema.

Restructuring procurement requires an open forum of communication with your key suppliers in order for the players in each pair to make clear their expectations, their experiences to date, their expectations for the future, and some understanding of the efforts expended versus the results received. Let us examine another example—a positive one.

At one time, Procter & Gamble assigned two dozen of its smartest people to work full time at Wal-Mart. Together they created many breakthroughs, including "cross-docking," a joint way of working in which P&G shipments are determined directly from actual sales in specific Wal-Mart stores so that these shipments never go into stock in Wal-Mart warehouses: They enter the warehouses in exact sequence so that they immediately go out to the stores—they simply "cross the dock." But this was only the beginning for the collaboration. Some 25 to 30 P&G people have continued to work with their counterparts at Wal-Mart. The question is always "what should we do next?" It is essential to focus on this kind of question—not the zero-sum thinking of classic purchasing.

✔ Even if you win the rat race, you are still a rat!

Separating the sheep from the goats

Chapter 1 described collaborative relationships with suppliers as comprising a minority of all suppliers, and further segmented this group into a small group of partners and even smaller group of "super-collaborative suppliers. It is the small set of super-collaborative relationships that we term "pairs of aces." These ideas can now be seen as Figure 3.1 (overleaf). At the base of the pyramid depicted in Figure 3.1, we have the rottweiler treatment of suppliers, then what we call "collaboration light," then partnerships, and finally pairs of aces.

The collaboration farm club

Depicting the supply base as shown in Figure 3.1 allows us to develop an evolutionary approach to collaboration. In some ways, the three cooperative relationship segments can be seen as a "farm club." There should be a natural evolution with collaborative suppliers: Good results in one level will tend to lead to development at another level. This is depicted by the two-headed arrow on the right-hand side of Figure 3.1—a supplier should be able to

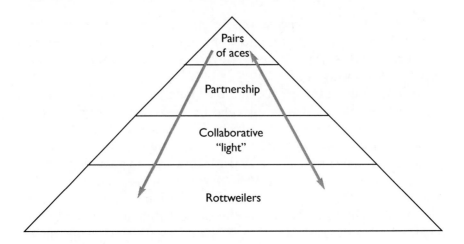

Figure 3.1 Supplier segmentation

move from one level to the next, and perhaps it might go the other way.

✔ All marriages are not made in heaven, and a supplier partnership can fail for many reasons.

The downward headed arrow on the left of Figure 3.1 depicts the learning that can come from collaborative relationships, and how it might be cascaded to other supplier interactions. Figure 3.1 is consistent with the imperative to always focus on what is next. It also recognizes that not all players make it to the big leagues, and some major leaguers end up back in the minors; some collaborative relationships will not live up to their potential. Figure 3.1 also allows us to envision a "collaboration light" that might be less thoroughly applied to a larger group of suppliers, perhaps reducing the combative segment. Bombardier Transport is currently attempting to do just this—applying a less intensive version of the supplier partnering approach to a wider group of suppliers.

The major lesson from Figure 3.1 is that within the collaborative set, the work progresses uniquely for each customer–supplier pair, with collaboration tending to follow the pattern described in Chapter 2, flawless execution, total cost of ownership (TCO), value/cost, and strategic alignment.

The largest portion of the collaborative relationships will involve joint efforts focused on flawless execution, usually to better integrate supply chain planning. The pairs labeled partnership have moved beyond the basics, now concentrating on TCO and perhaps extensions into value cost. It is these customer–supplier pairs that yield major win–win benefits, where concentration of the supply base makes sense, and where joint efforts improve standardization. The super-collaborative (pairs of aces) are where joint performance is being truly optimized—and perhaps where future improvements can be achieved through better strategic integration.

The customer–supplier pairs in the section labeled "partnership" imply a higher standard of collaborative work, one in which there is open communication of goals, development of shared values, and a series of joint improvement efforts. In essence, this is the supplier development R&D activity. It is with this group that integrated supply chain planning and other innovations will be first developed, before simplifying them and rolling them out to the other collaborative relationships.

Collaborative differentiation at Nokia

Nokia has developed an approach to evolution with suppliers based on degrees of collaboration. Figure 3.2 (overleaf) shows the company's model, as a 3x3 matrix. The suppliers are divided into multiple, single, and sole. This reflects whether there is more than one supplier (multiple) as well as if, in the case of one supplier, this supplier is the only one supplying the item (sole), or Nokia has *chosen* to buy only from this supplier but has other options (single).

The Y axis depicts the suppliers as furnishing items either locally to Nokia, across a geographical region, or globally to all Nokia factories. The most interesting feature of the Nokia supplier matrix is that when the relationship with a supplier shifts from one cell in the matrix to another, it mandates a transformation in the relationship between Nokia and the supplier (doing different things in each company—not just the same things better). A new relationship is required every time, and the supply chain needs to reflect the new reality and requirements for new information/coordination activities. The general progression is toward regional/global coverage with single-source suppliers.

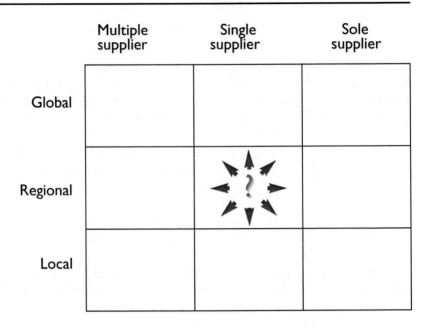

Figure 3.2 Nokia's supplier matrix

These are chosen for a model series, and thereafter evaluated on several criteria to see if they can/will be retained for the next model series of mobile phones.

Supplier lock-on may be the best game in town

Achieving a dominant position with your customers is certainly something desirable. It is great to establish lock-on with customers or incumbency, either where there are no substitutes for your products or where the relationship you have built with key customers is ironclad. This condition can be achieved through monopoly, through superior design, through moving up the value chain with an improved bundle of goods and services, or though the customer's ignorance. Fundamentally, long-run lock-on requires doing things better than the competitors—delivering better value/cost.

However, supplier lock-on can be equally important. Nokia over the years has definitively done this. At numerous times, its competitors have been unable to produce mobile phones because of a shortage of some key item but this is rarely the case for

Nokia. The company has intelligent arrangements with its suppliers, and has been very well aware of problems before they have become significant. At one time, Philips was making a particular integrated circuit for mobile phones in a US plant that suffered a fire. Nokia learnt of the fire within 24 hours, and before another 24 hours had passed, the company president—plus key people from the supply-chain organization—had met with the president of Philips and several of his key executives. Nokia came with an exact plan for what it would do and for what it wished Philips to do. The plan was agreed on and executed, and several weeks later, the competing mobile phone companies had to shut down production of phones with this component.

Be the most attractive customer

Collaboration is not easy. There is a history of more nonsense than partnership. Finally, the really good suppliers—those that can hold up their end in a pair of aces—will be in demand. This means that you as a customer need to be seen as more attractive than other choices for the best—smartest—suppliers. They too will be limited by the rule of ten, and you need to be at the top of their list. It is absolutely essential to identify what is in a partnership for both the customer and the supplier. That is the only way that realistic objectives can be set and true progress periodically assessed. You, acting as a customer, must explicitly determine what you will do to make your firm more attractive to your key suppliers. Moreover, you need to play the same game with those customers with which you wish to establish collaborative relationships. At the end of the day, it is essential that your suppliers *know* that you are their most important customer and that the relationship pays off—for them.

✔ Putting lipstick on a pig doesn't improve its looks.

Increasing attraction must not be seen as attained through providing higher prices to suppliers or lower prices to customers. This route will lead only to tougher negotiations and the problems associated with commodities, as discussed in Chapter 1. The right alternative is to become a "smart partner," one with which customers and suppliers wish to work because they gain important learning, and because the relationship moves into the advanced stages of cooperation, with significant joint benefits. But this requires a different set of skills and an improved basis for inter-firm communications.

> ✔ Purchasing managers are not particularly good at knowing whether their companies are attractive customers or at identifying how suppliers judge their companies' attraction.

We have found several suppliers with quite negative opinions about their "comfort" in working with a customer, while the purchasing manager in that firm thinks the suppliers find his company very attractive. This lack of alignment is fairly common, and needs to be rooted out. This can never be done completely, but having widely divergent opinions of a supplier (or customer) can be a serious problem.

We once asked several managers in a large consumer products company their opinion of a supplier of aluminum foil—and came up with strikingly different answers. The purchasing manager stated that the supplier was unreliable, with marginal quality, but cheap. The quality manager said that the supplier had OK quality but performed poorly on delivery. The operations manager denied any problems with either quality or delivery service. Bringing all of these opinions together allowed the consumer products company to abandon a plan to replace the foil supplier with another.

A similar problem often occurs in determining what makes a supplier attractive to a customer. The most common response is innovation. Most customers prefer their key suppliers to be actively working on innovative solutions, but suppliers often lament that innovative suggestions are poorly received, particularly when they are suggested to purchasing people. The purchasing people are continually being pushed to reduce prices of purchased items, so innovation proposals are often seen as disruptive to their hardball negotiations.

> ✔ Combative procurement is not interested in innovation.

Separating drivers from passengers

A critical end objective for working better with suppliers is to jointly develop a low-cost structure that allows the customer to compete better than its rivals. This means that suppliers will need to provide materials at lower cost, and suppliers that can do so are, naturally, viewed as attractive. But there is a fundamental difference between price reductions that are based on negotiating muscle and those based on joint efforts by the customer and supplier to engineer costs out of the chain. The suppliers who are ready and willing to engage in these joint cost reduction efforts are *truly* attractive, but this is a two-way street: The customer needs to invest time and energy in changing the inter-firm processes. The cost reductions well may come from improvements on the customer side.

Customers also regard suppliers as attractive if they supply leading-edge customers, are not overly dependent on one customer, and (obviously) run highly productive operations. Smart customers make periodic visits to supplier factories where they assess flawless execution, productivity, use of state-of-the-art practices, and general level of employee involvement in continuous improvement—for example, use of innovative quality programs. But suppliers can and should do the same thing. Your customers should operate at high levels of productivity and be smart competitors. Otherwise, you may have to subsidize them in their ability to compete.

Key point: If your suppliers are incurring extra costs, you pay for them. How many times have you visited factories where expensive equipment stands idle? This is a cost that will be borne by the end customers, one way or another. The benchmark here needs to be based on overall equipment effectiveness (OEE), which measures capacity utilization against a 24/7/52 standard. If you, working with the supplier, can increase OEE, both of you can reap the benefits.

The attraction of a supplier often depends on the customer organization's priorities of the moment. When Numico was ramping up capacity at a new factory in Poland, the factory team and other managers focused on substantially increasing production capacity. The most attractive suppliers for Numico were those able to keep up with the increasing demand while creating no problems for the factory. Attractive suppliers were those that were invisible, working so reliably that they required no time or attention.

Attraction depends on particular managers' objectives and the specific challenges they face, on the customer strategy, and the specific issues of the day.

   But now let's turn to the other side of this issue: What makes you, as a customer, most attractive? How can you convince the smartest suppliers to work with you?

Ten golden rules for becoming an attractive customer

1. **Be a demanding customer.** Challenge your suppliers, but don't crush them. If hard-hitting negotiation is the only tool in your bag, you have problems. Attraction does pay off, but you need to check opinions with key suppliers: Do *they* see you as only pushing prices?
2. **Determine which suppliers are important.** Attraction is not to be spread around like so much peanut butter. Identify which partnerships will pay off in the long term, and invest in them.
3. **Recognize—explicitly—that attraction is double-edged.** You will need to work hard to be seen as your key suppliers' most attractive customer. This also implies joint improvement efforts, not unilateral demands for the supplier to make them.
4. **Increase the supplier's comfort level.** Make sure that supplier managers know their ideas are welcomed, acknowledged, and implemented. Make it easy for them to provide them. Be fair and scrupulously honor contractual obligations.
5. **Help the supplier properly evaluate its expected payoffs.** A typical negotiation technique is to hide information. In fact, keeping information from key suppliers leads to poor evaluation and diminished attraction—of both customer and supplier.
6. **Manage the misalignment.** It is virtually impossible to align the objectives of purchasing, manufacturing, R&D, finance, and other functions. It is even more critical to understand and manage misalignment between the partners.
7. **Manage the perceptions.** Understand that it is perceptions that matter, and that these are often totally unrelated to reality. Proactively manage the "stories" and "feelings" about a supplier.
8. **Understand and manage how the supplier allocates resources and ideas.** Develop the reputation of being the most open customer to new ideas, by accepting as many as possible and

implementing them. Develop metrics that support implementing supplier ideas, and reward those in your company who do so.

9. **Help your suppliers leverage the learning.** If you not only allow but deeply encourage your suppliers to use the learning with their other customers, you will increase attraction and be the place where new learning is focused.

10. **Sell the opportunities in your company to the supplier**, and understand which other customers and initiatives are in the priority list of the supplier. You want to be at the top of it.

Every one of these ten golden rules applies equally well as a supplier in terms of what you need to do to become the most attractive choice for those key customers you wish to have. In fact, it is important to always look at both sides of the buying/selling relationship: What does the other person see as most attractive? How can our firm be the most attractive customer? The most attractive supplier?

Setting the improvement agenda

You cannot easily change combative procurement people into collaborative professionals (maybe never) and it certainly presents a great difficulty. Creating a procurement function able to develop the pairs of aces is a tough job, not to be underestimated. It is important to choose the directions early and to select/develop the procurement personnel/culture that matches your long-run needs. This implies a segmentation of procurement people as well as segmentation of the suppliers. Placing the wrong ones in the wrong places can lead to a situation like that of General Motors in Chapter 1. Similarly, fielding procurement personnel with the wrong mandates can be equally disastrous.

In October 2006, Collins & Aikman Corp. stopped deliveries to Ford Motor Co. because of a pricing dispute on instrument panels, carpeting, and interior parts. This was a highly unusual action by a supplier of this size, but indicative of the growing hostility in the industry. A Ford spokesman said, "The relationship has been irreparably harmed." Perhaps the company should look at itself instead of blaming the supplier.

In another example, Publicis recently hired a well-known procurement professional but constrained her initial actions to procurement of "non-strategic categories," with the promise that if this went well, Publicis would then allow her to purchase strategic items. This approach was fundamentally flawed, since the best approach to buying non-strategic items is largely combative, as are both the type of people who can do a good job and the measure of effectiveness (unit price reduction).

Get the right benchmarks

Perhaps one of the most bankrupt ideas in procurement is the single-minded focus on year-to-year unit price reduction. The Ford–Honda example cited in Chapter 1 clearly shows how that can work out: Ford is fat and happy accepting a modest price increase but beating the Consumer Price Index by 4 percentage points over a six-year period. In the meantime, Honda has *lowered* its prices by 19 percent. The moral of the story is that the unit price needs to be a passenger—not the driver. The Ford–Collins & Aikman story is similar. Here we have parts uniquely designed for Ford. Its benchmark is unit price, while those of Collins & Aikman are return on investment, cash flow, and the bottom line. There is no win–win in this relationship.

The key *drivers*, rather than passengers, need to be part redesign, standardization, substitute materials, improved supplier capacity utilization, simplified/coordinated actions, and benchmarking on what the Collins & Aikman parts "should cost." The "should cost" measure needs to be based on *optimal* rather than existing: design, manufacturing methods, capacity utilization, logistics, and coordinated planning. What could be the ultimate best way to create not just this part but the function it fulfills? This needs to be the benchmark to which current prices are compared, and through which *joint* improvement efforts (not unilateral demands) become prioritized.

Cost measures can be based on analytical models for how a part should be made and what its resultant cost should be. A less elegant but equally important process is a variant of managing by walking around. The smart companies such as Toyota have engineers who visit huge numbers of factories every year—the best ones—to see how things are done and what ideas they can glean. But again, a word of caution:

✔ There is a big difference between professional benchmarking and industrial tourism.

Let us be clear on an important issue in all of this: Establishing the "should-cost measure," prioritizing improvements, making the choice for improvement efforts, and, most importantly, achieving the results cannot be expected from classic procurement organizations. As noted in Chapter 1, if you own a dog and want a cat, no amount of kicking the dog will do the job.

Focus on total costs in the chain

Another way to think outside the box is for the senior executives in the customer–supplier pair to mandate development of total cost of ownership (TCO). TCO focuses attention on the product in use, not just its original purchase price. Although not easy to estimate exactly, in some cases ballpark estimates are good enough to prove the point. It is often the case that certain product features might be more costly initially but result in significantly lower maintenance costs and products that have longer life. This sounds completely logical but is often not the case in real life. In Chapter 1, we mentioned train manufacturer Bombardier Transport. BT's customers are typically governmental train operating units in various countries. Bids for new rail equipment are compared by a specialized group between one manufacturer and another. But if BT were to install better doors and/or a new variety of air compressor, the downstream maintenance—as well as the percentage of time the train was unavailable for passenger service—could be significantly reduced. As long as the personnel who buy the trains are not the same as those who service them, there is little hope for improvement in this situation. But if BT and the customer mandate a TCO approach, then perhaps they can cut through the fog.

None of this is easy, but it is better to measure the right thing approximately than the wrong one exactly.

So how do you achieve results here? How should cost measures and TCO be put into practice? What can you do to overcome the barriers? The answer must again start with partnerships. There are some customers/suppliers with which you can work and some for which there is no way to break existing practices. There are some for which senior managers can jointly cut through the current ways of working and some for which this is just not possible. In the end, this is simply another issue in customer/supplier segmentation, and evolution in collaborative relationships.

The first order of business is to separate the sheep from the goats; find the partners that have the right mindsets. Foster these relationships. We have had remarkable success in helping customer–supplier pairs to break out of what everyone saw as pure zero-sum games. Acting as objective third parties, paid equally by both supplier and customer, we find it necessary to examine the past, expose the skeletons in the closet, and find ways to benefit from reducing conflict. Thereafter, it is possible to lay out the key issues that need to be resolved and—more importantly—help the pair to understand the potential to be obtained through joint actions. Finally, this leads to a joint action program, timetable, and set of evaluative metrics.

The other side to concentrating volume as a customer for your key suppliers is in helping your customers to do the same for you. (Be sure to measure this!) The arguments are equally valid. You wish for your key customers to see the wisdom in single-sourcing to *your* firm. Implied here is a concomitant need for the customers to feel comfortable with this arrangement, and you must not underestimate the implications for your company. Flawless execution and surprises only for birthdays are the base; backup processes, contingency planning, risk reduction, and transparency are the next requirements. Finally, you as a supplier should initiate joint projects so that the pair can capture the potential benefits of sole-source supply.

Treat suppliers with "tough love"

It is essential that no one mistake the push for collaboration as being softhearted (or soft-headed) over the ongoing need for unit price reductions. Some of these gains should come from combative procurement, but the most important improvements will come from jointly taking cost out of the chain. Collaboration and partnering with suppliers does not in any way mean giving in to price increases, or an end to demanding price decreases. The difference is that these improvements can best be achieved through joint actions rather than through unilateral demands. The key point is: You want collaboration, but you need to be demanding. The demands are on both you and the supplier. If not, either of you might become complacent. This would lead to the collaboration becoming a competitive liability rather than an asset. We are always surprised when suppliers believe that collaboration means no price reduction. The two companies need to work together to reduce costs: A lion's share of the cost reduction needs to go to the customer so it can in turn compete more effectively with its competitors. The goal, however, in every collaborative situation should be in every case to at least maintain the supplier's margins.

This is similar to the relations established with key managers and employees in your company: you collaborate and establish stretch objectives and challenging targets. If you are not demanding enough, you create complacency; if you are excessive, you create anxiety, which could lead to a valued employee leaving the company or, in the case of a supplier, ceasing to be an attractive customer.

Figure 3.3 visualizes the likely performance that you can expect from suppliers, depending on the pressure (or, put more positively, motivation) put on the supplier and the team from your company. If you apply excessive pressure, you will become unattractive, and the supplier will reduce its efforts and try to exit the relationship. If there is very little pressure, the customer–supplier team may become complacent. Of course, as is true of employees, some collaborative efforts need no external pressure to deliver high performance—they apply it themselves.

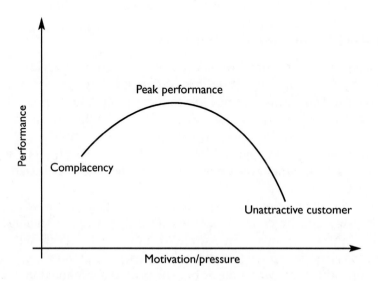

Figure 3.3 Motivation/pressure versus performance

✔ Tempted to increase pressure? Remember Isaac Newton's third law: "For every action, there is an equal and opposite reaction."

For employees, with too much pressure the probability of leaving increases substantially. In the case of suppliers, the result can be decreased interest in your business, less resources devoted, or even, as with General Motors, announcing that they will no longer supply.

"Tough love" in a collaborative relationship implies respecting, nurturing, valuing, and sharing. The demands are high on the supplier, but they are not unilateral. The pressure must be equally demanding on the customer side. The shared goal is to constantly improve and continually outperform the competition. You as a customer should greatly encourage your suppliers to challenge your present operations. They have other customers and visit many places. Do not only be open to new ideas and challenges of your operations—demand them.

A key question here is, why aren't these qualities (respect, nurture, value, sharing) more widespread? What limits them, and why do they wither on the vine? Our conclusion is that functional silos, narrow performance evaluations, and short-term horizons are the primary culprits. These exist in all firms: Senor managers need to find ways to first recognize them, and then offset them.

There are big bucks in standardization

A corollary to concentration is the need for standardization. Your company does not buy just dollars or euros, it buys specific things. There are enormous savings in reducing the number of those things. This is hard work that procurement people cannot accomplish. In most cases, there is a need to have marketing and engineering deeply engaged. Moreover, these efforts almost always involve a fundamentally new relationship with at least one supplier.

Unilever at one time had approximately 300 different wrappers for its Magnum ice-cream bar. It wasn't only different languages—packaging equipment in some plants was designed for polypropylene wrappers, while others used aluminum foil, etc. Everyone knew this was a mess, but the problem remained unsolved until the division manager told his staff, "I no longer want to hear why this cannot be done, I only want to hear from each of you what *you* are doing to get it done." Implementation required changes in packaging equipment and other operational issues. More critically, Unilever's marketing people had to decide on a uniform color for vanilla ice cream. Finally, consolidated procurement was implemented. The resultant cost reduction was substantial, but a much more important benefit was achieved. The first summer after the consolidation was cold in northern Europe and hot in the South. For the first time, product could be shipped north to south, instead of holding inventory in cold storage for a year while simultaneously facing stock-outs.

Standardization and modularity are often best achieved through collaborative design efforts with key customers and suppliers. Bombardier Transportation is again a good example. BT is working with Knorr-Bremse, the largest supplier of brakes and braking systems, to develop modular platforms of braking products that can be adapted to many new train designs, instead of taking each of these as a stand-alone project. This approach obviously results in lower costs and improved designs, but it also leads to cross-company integration of processes, reductions in contractual requirements, and communications focused more on win–win and less on negotiation.

Perception-based measures

There is always a passionate interest in measures and key performance indicators, and in which ones should be used for evaluating suppliers. To some extent, this is a search for the Holy Grail, since no measure is free of problems. But fundamentally, there is a problem in the basic thinking—it tends to be one-sided, with little thought for win–win.

✔ "Evaluating a supplier partner" is about as productive as "evaluating your spouse."

There has to be another way, and adding more measurements is not it. Furthermore, the measures for each pair need to be as different as the way you think about various family members. Each partnership will have different issues, with differing needs for improvement—and evaluation that will best focus attention. In the end, the most important issues come down to perceptions: How do the key players in the pair of companies *feel* about some issues? In almost all cases, we have observed that measures based on perceptions lead to better understanding of key issues and earlier identification of problem issues. The feelings are the drivers, or leading indicators, and the concrete measures are the passengers, or lagging indicators. Perception-based metrics can be straightforward, easy to collect, pair-based (both views of the situation), relatively easy to analyze, and supportive of periodic (time-series) analysis.

✔ As we've noted: It is better to be approximately right than exactly wrong.

There is also a tendency to erroneously believe that concrete numbers are superior to perception-based metrics. We described the problems with alignment above, but you might think they would be ameliorated with concrete measures. This is not the case. One of Bombardier Transport's important suppliers is a highly specialized contract manufacturing company called Enics. It focuses on supplying electronic items for small-series production and long life cycle products. This is exactly the situation for BT, since repair parts for trains are needed over long time horizons in small numbers. Enics has a factory in Switzerland and another in Sweden, and at one time, the on-time delivery performance for the two factories was 95 percent and 80 percent. But the Swiss plant—with the much better performance—was the one causing problems for BT: "The other 5 percent is the stuff we desperately need." In Sweden, if some item was a problem, the two firms worked out a joint solution with minimal effort.

So what?

Overhauling your procurement activity may well offer the single best way to improve your company's profitability and overall competitiveness. This is not an easy task, and it will not be a success if simply put on the shoulders of your existing purchasing organization. Major changes are called for in:

- the ways your company works with different supplier segments
- the ways they work with you

- the choice of personnel you assign to particular suppliers
- the mentality of your approach to working jointly with partner suppliers
- the establishment of clear wins for the suppliers
- the choices made for with which suppliers you will work intensively
- the objectives you need to set and your role in achieving them
- establishing the right benchmarks
- the mindsets of many players in your company
- the ways these players interact with different supplier segments
- the ways progress is measured and people are evaluated
- the appreciation and measurement of perceptions on both sides of the partnership
- the ways to establish and maintain objectives
- the leadership that you have to provide.

This chapter has focused on the transformational changes required in procurement in order to generate the power of two payoffs for your company. In Chapter 4, we turn to the other side of the coin: what is the transformation required in selling?

CHAPTER 4

Selling the way your customers *want to buy*

In Chapter 1, we put forward this book's fundamental proposition: The power of two firms (a customer and supplier pair) working in close collaboration is the best way to win today's tough competitive game. Chapter 2 expanded on the idea of collaboration, identifying four distinct stages, the efforts required to reach each of these stages, and the potential benefits to both customer and supplier of doing so. In Chapter 3, we examined the changes required in the ways a company buys. How does the customer need to adapt its procurement practices to work collaboratively with a small number of carefully selected suppliers?

This chapter deals with the other side of the coin: the changes needed in selling. You need to clearly understand the tough procurement policies and ideas that drive today's purchasing agenda. It is critical for a supplier to not be naïve about what is possible, with whom it might be able to work, and how to evolve sales/marketing plans accordingly. In Chapter 5 we expand these ideas, focusing on more revolutionary ideas in sales and marketing, and how these need to be integrated with some key customers to create significant win–win results.

A fragrance company was trying to create a unique selling proposition for one of its most important customers, in an effort to help the customer differentiate its products and services. The fragrance company was able to sell this concept to the customer's marketing and research executives but clashed with the purchasing managers over prices and was unable to recover its investment in innovation and services. Price was the only issue on which the buyers would focus.

Train manufacturers often proposes a total-cost-of-ownership approach to train operators. Again, the "concept" may be well accepted, but in most countries, the train buyers are evaluating solely on initial prices, not on subsequent maintenance costs.

Lafarge, the large French building materials company, can sell plaster-board of different qualities. It is purchased by construction companies which opt for cheaper materials, while the building owner wants more durable ones.

A food additives firm wished to sell both an additive and a flavor to one of its large yogurt customers. But the yogurt manufacturer saw the two items as different "commodities"; they were purchased independently by different buyers.

In most companies, buyers are evaluated on period-to-period unit price reduction. Trying to sell them value/cost makes sense only when the cost is going down (resulting in lower prices) – the numerator in this ratio has little value to them personally.

Business-to-business selling is different

Selling to businesses is not the same as selling to consumers. The experiences from selling consumer products cannot be directly transferred to business-to-business situations. It may be better to forget many marketing theories, such as the famous five Ps or six Ss. What is truly good for the customer in terms of helping it achieve better long-term results is often impossible to sell; there are too many built-in barriers.

In many business-to-business (B2B) environments, your sales-people are not truly selling. rather, it is professional buyers from the customer companies who buy your products and services. These professionals are equipped with sophisticated tools and a deep knowledge of your cost structure, your manufacturing productivity, alternative sources, and comparative benchmarks. The result is a much better understanding of the supplier's economic situation than most suppliers are willing to believe. Moreover, these rottweilers are unimpressed by sales arguments that focus on abstract issues such as research capabilities. In fact, they will tell you to quit spending money on these things and give them the savings.

Selling to purchasing experts

The CEO of the fragrance company mentioned above concluded that its customer invested more in training its purchasing managers than the fragrance company did in training its salespeople. The net result was customer managers more knowledgeable and better equipped to win in the inevitable price negotiation battles.

✔ Equipping the fragrance salespeople to sell "solutions" and "total cost of ownership" was like sending cavalry to fight tanks.

In the majority of B2B environments, you need to sell the way the customers are set up to buy. Forget about the way you *want* to sell, your fantastic unique selling proposition, your "value added" services or products, your "solution," and your platinum, gold, and blue service levels. These may be truly great ideas—ones that would truly help your customers. But in most cases, the buyer is going to tell you exactly the goods, the integration, and the service he or she wants. These people are not enfranchised to "change the rules of the game."

BT makes a "bogie" (the wheels, brakes, and undercarriage of a train car) that costs 10 percent more but has lower operating costs that offset the higher price in less than five years. These bogies have a lifespan of 30 years, but they can be sold only in the United Kingdom, where BT takes on the downstream maintenance costs as well as original equipment costs.

In an increasing number of situations, your salespeople face buyers with MBA degrees, better knowledge of your cost structure than your accounting department, and better understanding of your company's strengths and weaknesses than your board of directors. Furthermore, they are charged with one and only one objective – to get prices down. This is the way today's purchasing professionals conduct their work. They dissect your sales proposition with scientific precision, taking only the most interesting pieces and demanding elimination of all superfluous ones. They are experts in negotiation and in extracting the most value from your business; their job is to commoditize your industry.

When these rottweilers have finished biting you, they do not hesitate to push the same aggressive approach on your suppliers. They can thereby leverage volumes they buy indirectly through tier-two suppliers, bypassing your own purchasing organization and seeking special concessions. They only have one objective in mind: Do better than their competitors at leveraging upstream resources (that is, lower prices from you and your suppliers).

These buyers have been trained in "reverse marketing," so they are immune to gimmicky offers. They X-ray your marketing strategy to take advantage of the real bargains rather than the special offers. Finally, when they taste the sweetness of a discount, they become addicted rebate sharks and drive your margins to historically low levels. Why all this?

✔ If these buyers do not bleed you dry, they will have a comparative disadvantage if their competitors do it.

It is important to recognize that a major revolution is occurring in purchasing. Table 4.1 illustrates the key trends; you—as a supplier—need to understand these and act accordingly. If the supply base for major customers is to decrease by 75 percent, how do you become one of the remaining 25 percent, and what will it mean for the ways you need to sell?

Smart financial analysts understand the impact of aggressive purchasing strategies on the future share price. They look for companies initiating programs called "Stretch," "Booster," or "Squeeze." These should reduce input costs–and increase profitability. Recently in

Table 4.1 New sales realities

Sales/marketing must reflect these new realities:

- Sell as customers wish to buy
- Leading-edge customers will reduce supply base
- Leading-edge customers will reduce number of items purchased
- Implication: major increase in average buy
- Fewer purchasing agents/fewer salespeople
- Negotiation more periodic – less continuous
- Expectations for new systems/logistics linkages
- Who will win the orders?
- How?
- New competencies required?

the fast-moving consumer goods industry, one company issued a profit warning because of increasing input cost (and quickly lost almost 10 percent of its market capitalization); while a competitor that was more efficient in purchasing saw its share price rise thanks to a cost control initiative.

- What could be a better illustration of the strategic importance of a well-run purchasing function?
- A few months ago, two major US companies merged, with a plan to slash costs by $16 billion. How much will be coming from suppliers? A significant portion, for sure.

Perhaps you should no longer wonder why your customers invest more money in training their purchasing people than your company does in developing sales professionals.

Purchasing is where the money is

All firms are looking for ways to improve their bottom-line performance. Many see improved purchasing as the answer.

✔ As 1930s outlaw Willie Sutton was (probably falsely) reported to have said when asked why he robbed banks, "Because that's where the money is."

The sheer amount of money a company pays to its suppliers and third parties makes this the biggest potential source of improvement. Total purchasing spend typically represents 65 percent of a manufacturer's average sales. With growing trends in outsourcing and offshoring, the total will soon reach as much as 80 percent. Furthermore, until the early 1990s, most companies made purchasing a low priority.

✔ There was—and still is—plenty of low-hanging fruit.

Many companies are transforming purchasing from a dull clerical activity into a strategic business activity. In recent years, these firms have completely changed the profile of people working in purchasing. They are well trained and receive continuous training updates. Measurement structures are well formulated (cost-focused), and day-to-day objectives are simple. These professionals increase their knowledge of supplier cost structures while in parallel increasing their power. In the end, they know the detailed structures of supplier businesses and end up being in the driver's seat. The business they represent becomes so indispensable that many suppliers evaluate requests from the customer purchasing organization at the board level.

✔ If these are your customers, you are in for "interesting times."

Leveraging purchasing spend in innovation

Recently, a leading food company's VP of purchasing explained a new way to leverage his supplier base. His company's annual procurement spend is around €800 million; it invests €50 million in research. Analysis of his suppliers' annual reports led to the conclusion that they invested around 6 percent of their revenue in research and development. Therefore, he contends, his company supports approximately €48 million for research in supplier companies—roughly equal to their internal R&D expenditure. He now demands to know: Are these funds invested for my benefit—or for my competitors'? What is my company concretely seeing as a return on its investment in my suppliers' R&D?

How would your company respond to such a question?

Sell the way your customers want to buy: "reverse purchasing"

Purchasing managers have learnt about marketing and selling tools by studying them; this is sometimes called "reverse marketing." Now sales and marketing managers must similarly learn the tools and techniques used by advanced purchasing professionals—and practice some degree of reverse purchasing. This is another classic form of knowing your customers. In consumer marketing, professionals study consumer behavior in terms of general shopping and purchasing habits, tastes, and spending potential. The difference is that in B2B, the specific purchasing professional in a particular company is the "animal" to study.

Do not assume that all purchasing professionals behave in exactly the same manner, or that all customers will perceive your company similarly. You need to understand the goals and approaches used by each of those that are key for you—and act accordingly.

You need to understand in detail the tools the purchasing manager has in their toolbox. In dealing with some purchasing managers, your salespeople need to be knowledgeable on reverse auctions, deep sourcing, value analysis, and target-costing methodologies. For each customer, they need to know how these are applied, and if/when/how you will participate in their application. Finally, you need to understand how your customers manage their supply chain, how they measure its effectiveness, and how they manage their cash—and yours.

It is useful to prepare for whatever game the purchasing manager proposes—and be ready to decline to play. Reverse auctions are a good example: They can be brutal, but if you have excess capacity and need business, you may be willing to engage. But you can also send signals to customers that you prefer to avoid this game because it is not in your long-term *joint* interests. This signal will reach the other players in the auction—where it will also have an effect.

What if your customer tries the gambit of offering transparency, asking for "open books"? Our recommendation is to say that this would be an excellent idea—when the relationship reaches the point where you and the customer can mutually benefit. If this is just a new form of negotiation, then you are not interested.

In short, you need to educate your sales executives in reverse purchasing. First, understand that many classic selling techniques are no longer appropriate; you must unlearn them. Second, you and your team need to study the latest approaches in how purchasing and supply chain managers work, which tools and strategies they use, and what motivates them. Third, you must do all you can to understand what metrics your customers are using, which ones are new, and how you stack up on those metrics. Finally, you should appreciate that networking, socializing, and spending time with your customers is still the best way to support reverse purchasing and, more importantly, to offset the worst features of cutthroat purchasing practices.

Yes, you heard it right: Playing golf or having a sauna or a good lunch with customers is a very important part of selling to businesses—understanding what they measure, why your performance is good and continually improving, and getting beyond selling commodities.

✔ Our earlier maxim still holds: If you are in the commodity business, you deserve it.

Selling to customer segmentation models

Reverse purchasing recognizes that the customer's approach to segmenting the market may be more important in defining the way you need to sell than your own segmentation model. Fundamentally, it is critical to understand how the customer views you—as a supplier. You may or may not be an *important* supplier. The decision is obviously linked to the sales volumes between the firms and their relative sizes, but there are other features as well, including key technology, historical relations, geography, and future potential.

A typical purchasing segmentation

Typically, purchasing professionals classify their suppliers along dimensions similar to the ones shown in Figure 4.1. A customer buys a high volume of products and services, or a low volume. High/low is from the buying company's perspective, not the supplier's. Additionally, the customer can classify its suppliers in terms of criticality of the product and/or service they provide. Critical might be paper for a newspaper printer; noncritical might be office paper for a fitness gym.

Using this matrix, purchasing managers classify their suppliers as:

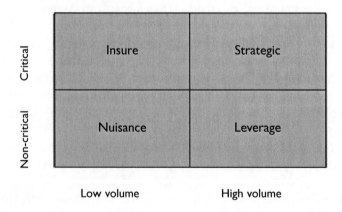

Figure 4.1 Segmentation of suppliers from a purchasing point of view

strategic (high volume and critical), insure (low volume and critical), leverage (high volume and non-critical), and nuisance (low volume and noncritical). The customer will shape its purchasing strategy accordingly.

- Relationships with *critical* suppliers should be on a partnership basis—no surprises, flawless execution, joint value/cost improvements, interest in new technology, joint processes.
- For *insure* suppliers, the customer will try to develop alternative sources and will aim to develop metrics that avoid surprises. Since volumes are low, detailed price negotiations may be less important.
- *Leverage* is where price squeezing reaches its peak. This is rottweiler land, where good purchasing managers earn their salaries.
- Finally, we have *nuisance*. Here the customer tries to get rid of the problem: Can we outsource this, combine it with something else, simplify it drastically, or find a substitute that has more potential for us?

By looking through this lens, it is obvious that developing a partnership with a customer that classifies your company as a nuisance simply will not work. The best strategy for dealing with these customers is to be as low-maintenance as possible and to minimize transaction costs.

If a customer classifies your product or service as a leverage opportunity, approaching that company for partnership is economic suicide, since it considers your product or service to be a commodity. Your only viable strategy is to offer the best prices by minimizing your services and "extras." The irony is that it is likely that this customer is an important one for your organization, and if so, you need to work hard to develop a low-cost structure. You can expect the customer to continually pick apart your cost structure, continually asking you to eliminate "waste," but you can and should push back: Charge that company postage for sending it a sample!

If your company and its products are deemed "insure," you may be in a nice position: Just keep quiet and charge good prices, since it is not worth the customer's trouble to hassle you. Additionally, increasing the switching costs for your goods and services will further insulate you from the rottweilers.

A great irony is that while you, as a supplier, try to differentiate your products and services—for example, moving them from leverage to strategic—your customer's purchasing organization is attempting just the opposite: to move high-volume items to the leverage box. Food for the rottweilers!

We often see examples of this. "Systems suppliers" provide problem solutions, but at some point the smart purchasing people add up the "should cost" estimates for all the individual items in the "system." This in turn leads to the customer buying these and becoming the systems integrator. The best defense against this move by a customer is first to understand that it well might happen, and then to work closely with the customer to continually enhance the bundle of goods and services you provide. Make sure the "system" is more than the sum of its parts; complacency is dangerous.

It is critical that as a supplier of systems solutions you continually assess the "value added" of your system. Furthermore, you need to clearly communicate this value added to the customer, and refine it based on the customer's input. In the final analysis, your value added must best support your customer's value proposition—or the one that it is trying to create for *its* customers.

If you are classified as a strategic supplier, you may have opportunities to develop the relationship further—into a partnership and true win–win relationship. Doing so requires joint commitment and understanding that need to be nurtured over time. Finally, if you are a strategic supplier, you must help create a customer–supplier team to manage and continuously enhance your value added as it supports the customer objectives. Why is the total more than the sum of the parts? Where is the intellectual property? Are you reducing risk in some way?

Understand the games you need to play

A major objective of this chapter is to emphasize the predominant behavior of the latest purchasing methods and approaches: They are tough, and there are limited opportunities to change them. But knowing them for what they are is important. As a supplier, you need to understand how your customers view you:

- Do they use a matrix such as Figure 4.1?
- If so, where do you fit in it?

- Is there any chance of changing your position?
- Forewarned is forearmed.

There is no point being naïve about how your customers want to buy from you. In addition, you need to know how the particular purchasing manager is evaluated in his or her company. Changing the focus is often just not feasible in the short run, and you need to carefully determine whether long-run efforts can achieve desired results. Knowing what tools a particular company's purchasing professionals are using allows you to search for feasible ways to respond. Your strategy must include responding to the purchasing manager's expectations and needs, in order to become a more important and valued supplier in his or her eyes. This is a minimal requirement; without it, you will become an ex-supplier to this customer. However, you also need to take a hard look at the relationship. If it has no possibility of developing beyond one of total customer dominance, perhaps it is time to work with other customers. Many automobile suppliers have clearly reached this decision with regard to the US big three auto manufacturers.

One part of the game is to recognize that your customer is not just the purchasing manager. While some managers will do their best to keep you from other company contacts, as a supplier you will often deal with multiple contacts in a customer company, with different policies, key performance indicators, and motivations. In order to change the situation, you will almost surely need to find ways to interact with others in the customer organization—those who can appreciate total cost of ownership and value/cost.

It is very likely that the purchasing manager you face is evaluated on price reductions, that the marketing or research manager is interested in ideas for new or enhanced products, and that the logistics and production executives are interested in reliability and trouble-free operations. A key question for you is whether any of this matters—or *can* matter.

✔ Are you locked into being a "leverage," "nuisance," or "insure"?

Even if you can get beyond unit price as the sole criterion of evaluation, there is still the question of whether you should put more emphasis on service, new product development, or cost. Still others

tomer company might well be pushing for flexibility. Your
eeds to focus on each of these key customers and how to
ir offer to their way of buying.

If—and for most suppliers this is a big if—you do have the possibility of changing the game with a few customers, you will have
work accordingly. You need to know how your customer's decision
makers are evaluated, and how your sales proposition to that particular customer can help each of these key managers to be more
successful; you also need to help them develop a composite view of
what you provide to their company. It is much easier for a customer
to find a better supplier in terms of one single criterion than on
many. Figure 4.2 shows how suppliers can—in some situations—
compete on more than price. The chart also indicates another issue:
This is hard work. You need to choose wisely with which customers
to work. Where can a "pair" be developed into a true win–win?

What do customers want from key suppliers?

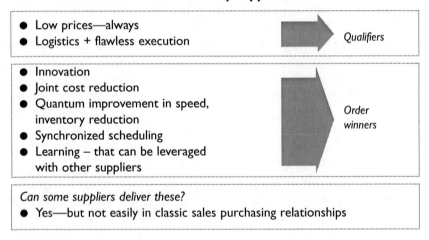

Figure 4.2 A customer–supplier relationship based on more than price

Figure 4.2 looks nice, but another key problem is that most
customers lack good ways to put all this together. The result is
misalignment in terms of the way the supplier is evaluated. There
will always be different perceptions about the desirability of
working with a given supplier, in the various functional areas of the

customer. These cannot be eliminated—they can only be understood and managed as best as possible. Key people in both the customer and supplier company need to manage the misalignment.

One final observation. Problems of misalignment will be unique to each customer–supplier relationship—and must be managed accordingly. The problems are different, the perceptions reflect historical events, and the people who must resolve the issues are always unique as well. You cannot have a general strategy for dealing with your customers; you will need to develop a "mass customization" approach to the way you manage customer relations.

When the worm turns

Every so often, the dominant role of customers becomes eroded by events. For example, as a result of China's skyrocketing demand for raw materials, a series of companies had to stop production because of a lack of supplies. Nissan, for one, was planning factory shutdowns because of a steel shortage. Suppliers were actually giving preference to other customers over Nissan and its suppliers.

We remember the joy of a manager of an iron ore company explaining how his company was canceling deliveries to a Japanese steel manufacturer: "Three years ago, they took advantage of us, making us sign an almost money-losing contract. Now we are not renewing it."

These recent events and the relative shift in power positions have made purchasing professionals much more receptive to new initiatives. You—as a supplier—should use this opportunity to learn positively about your customers' sourcing strategies and to change them in a constructive way.

Key account management

There is a vast literature on key account management, and it is not our intent to repeat it here. Our focus now is to evolve from a focus on systems selling to one of enterprise selling. (For example, how does ABB move from selling turbochargers to Caterpillar to selling it robots, electrical equipment, and all the other ABB products of possible use? How can ABB sell the benefits of leveraging their collective competencies?) This is not an either/or issue, but enterprise selling focuses on selling significantly more to an existing customer. This is quite consistent with state-of-the-art procurement:

Many companies, such as Bombardier Transport, are deliberately reducing their supplier base and standardizing. The new game is to reduce significantly the supplier base and the number of items purchased, which implies a strong increase in the amount purchased per supplier.

One immediate issue this raises for a supplier is whether it will be one of the remaining suppliers—or an ex-supplier. It is not a brilliant idea to just wait to find out. Again, the direction here is coming from the purchasing (customer) side: It sees supply base reduction as a profitable route to travel. But what about the suppliers? Do you as a supplier sit back and wait, do you act proactively to help a key customer consolidate, or do you rethink the total set of relationships you might have with the right customer? That is—going back to stage 4 collaboration in Chapter 2—do you now jointly commit to developing the "white spaces" in this customer–supplier pair? Will this work? Have you progressed enough on collaboration stages 1–3 to support it?

For many suppliers, taking a proactive approach will involve significant internal change, market segmentation, and a selection of which customers might result in "pairs of aces." Is there a customer that can become a "super-customer—that is, what might you do with this customer to dramatically increase your business as well as the results from that business?

The choice often ends in assigning a key account manager (KAM) to each of these customers, but we see the challenges as much more encompassing than classic key account management. Making super-customer account management work well requires addressing two additional key challenges: centralization and coordination/synergy.

Centralization

Most firms have sales forces organized by geography and business units, each with its own set of objectives. Key account management (with a super-customer focus) adds several wrinkles to what is already complex.

- Does the KAM replace, lead, or "orchestrate" the existing sales force with the particular customer?
- Does key account management simplify or complicate life for

the existing set of inter-firm relationships? Synergy usually adds complexity.

- Can the KAM make deals? Does he or she negotiate with the customer?
- Can the KAM prioritize work in the operating business units?
- Can the KAM accept new business without approval of the operating business units?
- How does the KAM "sell" breakthrough ideas—internally as well as to the key account?

Coordination/synergy

A critical problem with key account management is how to coordinate the work across the business units, both inside the supplier and at the customer, and how to make the whole more than the sum of the parts. Each case will be somewhat unique, since the customers will have their own issues regarding centralized purchasing, differing evaluative criteria for businesses and geography, and differences in strategy.

Coordination inside the supplier company is at least as complex. The KAM needs to coordinate the customer's entire set of demands among the various divisions and business units. He or she will also have to negotiate with the internal units to create some kind of unified face to the customer. This will be doubly difficult when the business units use differing systems and processes. The key customer may not appreciate differing billing processes, duplication, and no consistent way to deal with the supplier.

The process is further complicated when systems solutions replace component/partial solutions. The systems integration work at the supplier will often require new cross-organizational processes. Project management becomes an increasingly important core competence.

Coordination with greatly expanded sales will increasingly need top management inputs. These will be required to set the standards for openness and collaboration—and also, increasingly, to deal with conflict resolution, project management, responsibilities for field failures, and price negotiations, now based on the overall business, not individual transactions.

The same kinds of complications and necessary changes exist on the customer side. Perhaps the buying is done by division, business unit, or commodity code (all steel, for example). The KAM needs to sell the ways in which the customer wishes to buy. Moreover, what may be synergistic for the customer company in total can easily be a nuisance for its individual operating units. This is particularly the case in the buying of non-product-related items, such as temporary labor, company cars, capital equipment, and advertising. In each of these cases, there are major potential savings for the customer in coordinated buying, but achieving these requires a significant degree of cooperation among business units. From the supplier side, key account management can be equally challenging: who sells to whom, how are the overall demands of the customer allocated to the supplier business units and geographies, how are prices set, and whose ox gets gored when the inevitable conflicts arise?

An interesting example we recently studied is the case of ABB implementing key account management—or, more correctly, re-implementing key account management, since it had been tried several times in the past, without success. We largely focused our studies on the ABB approach to implementing key account management with Caterpillar.

The main ABB product sold to Caterpillar is large turbochargers, for the company's marine engines and other large diesel engines. But the KAM's goal is to leverage these sales opportunities for additional ABB products. For example, if Caterpillar is building a new mining machine with traction motors to power it, this is a good potential customer for the ABB group that makes traction motors for other applications. But this requires that the KAM be aware that Caterpillar is indeed interested in this new activity, and that he or she is able to develop and nurture this relation in the appropriate places in both firms.

So how do ABB KAMs spend their time? How are their efforts evaluated? To whom should the KAM report? The Caterpillar KAM does not report to any ABB division, business unit, or geographical entity; instead, all KAMs report directly at the ABB group level. This enables them to work with the customer in whatever geographic area makes most sense, and with whatever customer business unit is appropriate. However, the KAM has no decision-making power—on prices or anything else—over an ABB business unit. This means that the KAM is essentially a coordination role, visiting Caterpillar locations, trying to understand that company's needs, and relating these to the various ABB business units that could satisfy these needs. This is not always a smooth process. There are times when this KAM has identified potential business opportunities but run into opposition at the business unit level: the business represented too much of a shift in the ABB unit's strategic orientation, a need to adapt its ways of operating, serious investments of capital and human resources, and a whole new set of sales issues.

ABB is continually searching for ways to improve its KAM process, but there is no doubt that is currently working well. In recent years, ABB has grown the business significantly faster with the KAM customers than with its other businesses.

The key questions that come from this example are how to choose what is best for a pair of closely collaborating companies (customer and supplier), and how to make decisions with a minimum of top-down *diktats*. At the end of the day, we again see the power of two: a major opportunity to enhance buying and selling.

None of this is easy, but if it were there would be no good jobs.

When customers change the game

A central tenet of this chapter is that purchasing is becoming ever more professional, and that you as a supplier must understand the resultant trends and changes in procurement behavior. For many firms, squeezing suppliers further is like trying to milk a stone. The fat is gone—and in far too many cases, so are the muscle and part of the bone. Suppliers need to make money. They need to invest in new equipment. They need to do R&D. They need to pay a fair return to their shareholders. Putting them out of business will hurt the customer as well.

Partnerships

The word *partnership* has a long history of misuse.

✔ Partnership is too often proposed to suppliers, when what results is instead better termed "partnerwhip."

"Partnerwhip" occurs when a customer proposes collaboration and win–win, but does not really mean it. It might even *think* it means it, but it is actions, not words that count. However, best practice in procurement now does embrace partnership. There is an understanding in leading-edge firms that improvements in purchasing prices are indeed still the best competitive game in town. But these need to be seen as passengers, where the drivers are partnership and carefully selected collaborative customer—supplier value/cost improvement efforts.

To some extent, the switch to partnership approaches has been driven by the shortage of materials described above. But a more fundamental development is a growing awareness that continuing with rottweiler approaches will inevitably reach an unsustainable point.

A few years ago, we worked with Mabe Estufas, a Mexican manufacturer of kitchen appliances. At one point, working in a joint venture with General Electric (GE), Mabe developed a very successful line of gas stoves for the US market. The venture was able to utilize many GE competencies, including a superior rottweiler approach to managing suppliers. Unfortunately, a new model series was more successful than planned, and Mabe was unable to increase parts deliveries from its suppliers. In essence, Mabe had squeezed the suppliers so hard that they had been unable to invest in new equipment, added capacity, or new product development. GE (correctly) blamed Mabe for the problems, and the company recognized its role. It needed to apologize for its past behavior, quickly help the suppliers to develop the necessary capacity, and fundamentally overhaul its purchasing organization and approach. Partnership became a genuine necessity, not a set of fancy words.

Making a definitive switch

We have discussed the procurement approach of Bombardier Transport (BT) several times. It too has an approach not dissimilar to that illustrated in Figure 4.1. BT has significantly reduced its supplier base, to approximately 1000, of which about 50 are seen as potential "partners." The company treats the other 950 with more or less classic procurement approaches. But within the group of 50 partners, there is a second group of 15 to about 20 suppliers that are considered *truly* strategic partners. BT sees the objective as forging true win–win partnerships with this group, in which BT is regarded as the favorite—most attractive—supplier, and each of these firms is in turn seen as a most attractive supplier. The result should yield BT a definitive competitive advantage. These are the company's potential pairs of aces.

Selecting the initial suppliers with the potential to become pairs of aces has been a relatively easy task. The selection has naturally included some of BT's largest suppliers, but it also has a few relatively small ones—each of which has special features of particular interest. For example, BT has singled out one small Polish company, because BT believes it is strategically important to develop low-cost country sourcing for the long haul.

The more difficult part of developing these key supplier relationships seems to be the "unlearning" that needs to take place in both BT and in each of the supplier firms. There is a natural degree of animosity that is based on past "war stories" and personal histories/biases. It is difficult for many people—in both the customer and the supplier companies—to truly put their cards on the table and trust that the result will be beneficial. Moreover, there is a reluctance to give up the classic negotiation games, in which contracts are dangled, then withheld, then renegotiated a few times.

An unusual approach to overcoming past history was recently implemented by Reckitt Benckiser, a leading UK manufacturer of cleaning and healthcare products. The company has worldwide operations and sales, and has shown strong growth in sales and earnings in recent years.

Reckitt Benckiser partially achieved its excellent financial results through tough purchasing methods and approaches. The company pushed its suppliers very hard—and achieved good results by doing so. But recently, it too came to the conclusion that this strategy would no longer be effective in light of significant increases in raw material and other input costs. It was time for a change to partnership, but how was this to be achieved? How could Reckitt Benckiser now pursue value/cost jointly with key suppliers? How could it break the mold created by its past behavior? How could the company change the attitudes and day-to-day practices of its procurement personnel?

Reckitt Benckiser sponsored a day-long event for its top 20 or so suppliers, initiating an extended discussion of why the company and its key suppliers now needed to adopt partnership. As a final touch, the participants were given a token of appreciation, in the form of a "break glass in case of emergency" fire alarm. Inside was a top of the line mobile phone. CEO Bart Becht told the group that the phones had one number already encoded on it—his mobile. Suppliers were told to call that number any time there was a problem with implementing the partnerships. One of the participants immediately pushed the appropriate button, and indeed Becht's phone rang. The subsequent impact inside Reckitt Benckiser was equally dramatic: any one of the suppliers could call the big boss—at any hour of the day or night.

So what?

Selling the ways in which customers (particular customers) wish to buy is essential. A "one size fits all" model does not work well in the B2B world. One major learning point is the need to understand the current best practices in procurement and to adapt your selling techniques accordingly. There is room to maneuver, but it is limited in most cases—and impossible in many. It is critical to allocate your collaboration resources to the right targets.

There is no point in trying to create a partnership with a customer that is interested only in beating down your sales prices. It is counter-productive and will leave you in a weaker position. You need to find out how best to respond to customer demands—and when to just say no. This is easier said than done, particularly in firms with ambitious sales growth objectives and periodic reporting of financial results. Unfortunately, if this is your situation, your customers will know it.

A key issue is finding the few customers for which the agenda can be expanded beyond unit price reduction. Selling as the customer wishes to buy can include providing innovation, speed, cash-flow improvements, top-line developments, and other issues. But this is only true when these wishes are real—not some disguised negotiation tactic. These can take place only in certain instances, usually requiring new avenues of communication. Do not expect that your salespeople will be able to pull this off by themselves.

The state-of-the-art in procurement is, however, changing. Smart firms now see that collaborative relationships with a small number of key suppliers can result in major win–win benefits, and these are long-run. If a key supplier has achieved superior results and good learning from working with your company, there is a potential loyalty—attractiveness—that can be leveraged in further collaborative efforts.

As a customer, then, you need to ask how much of your present approach to procurement is appropriate, whether at least some is obsolete, and where you might be able to leverage the power of two ideas. But you need to not underestimate the internal changes required to pull this off. The procurement people in your firm will need to "unlearn" some classic procurement concepts.

As a supplier, you also need to understand when things might be changing for a key customer: What are *its* challenges and strategic responses? How does this play out in *its* approach to procurement —and what might this mean for you? Moreover, you need to become proactive in this regard. Your salespeople can and should be able to identify the few customers who have the potential to change their ways. You need to understand their strategy—and how your company can help them win their competitive battles.

Chapter 5 picks up on these ideas. In this chapter we advocate a more proactive role for sales, where potential partnership-based customers can be identified and developed. The key messages are to break out of being mere "order takers," to support key accounts with deployment of key personnel, and to focus on developing your attraction as a supplier.

Choosing your battles wisely

Chapter 4 has a key message: You need to sell in the light of how your customers wish to buy, and not flog dead horses. You must expect that your customers will see procurement as a key source of profit improvement and develop the means to squeeze every possible drop of price reduction out of most suppliers. Being naïve as to their intentions, or believing in the "smoke" they generate, is not in your interest. Selling efforts need to be focused on where they can best pay off, but there is more to it than this:

- In far too many cases, salespeople are too timid.
- Sales is largely "order taking."
- There are insufficient efforts devoted to breakthrough efforts.
- Securing business is being left solely to salespeople.
- Plans are not developed to break out of rottweiler treatment.

Chapter 1 depicted the game for a customer in terms of its mix of supplier relationships. A similar set of ideas for segmenting the supplier base and allocating procurement resources was presented in Chapter 3. In Figure 5.1 we show the contrasting challenges presented to the supplier. When considering a customer, you need to expect that the vast percentage of its suppliers will be treated with a combative approach, with its procurement deployed accordingly. It will only be the few cases where collaborative approaches will be the customer's objective. Most suppliers will be treated badly, and for even those who are seen to be collaborative, there is a definitive hierarchy.

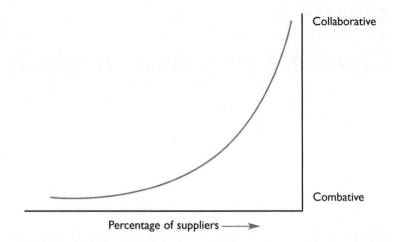

Figure 5.1 Procurement deployment

This implies that on one level, your selling organization needs to be similarly deployed. Defend your turf, and play the game wisely. Do not be fooled into wrong conclusions about your position.

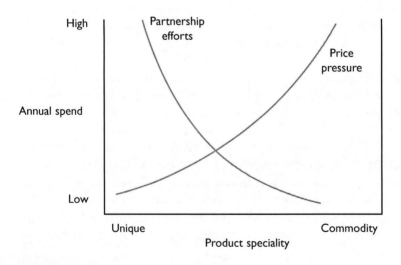

Figure 5.2 Product sourcing strategy

Figure 4.1 presented four supplier segments that a procurement function might use to partition its supplier base. Figure 5.2 depicts a related customer way of operating. The procurement organization should be expected to place your products somewhere between "unique" and "commodity," and it will also be aware of its annual spend on your products. If you sell it commodity products with a high annual spend, you need to expect great price pressure. If the amount it buys is small, you may be able to slip under the radar. If you have a unique product, and the annual spend is high, you should expect this customer to be interested in partnership efforts.

✔ But beware of the fox in sheep's clothing: Partnership or partnerwhip?

The lessons from these two figures are that you need to determine what the operational approach being used by each of your key customers is, and where you fit in this scheme. What will they try to do to you, and what is the appropriate response on your part?

Above and beyond developing a defense mechanism to counter aggressive price pressures by your customers, it is important to at least try to change your destiny.

- Who says you should be subjected to rottweiler treatment? How might you change this?
- What might you be able to offer that gets beyond "commodities"?
- To whom would you need to sell an enhanced bundle of goods and services, and who on your side would have to be involved?
- Why shouldn't your company be one selected for partnership treatment? What might you offer that is different?
- What should your sales force and others be learning about this customer?
- Who should be making contacts that get you beyond being chewed up by the rottweilers?

Proactive sales leadership

Figures 5.1 and 5.2 indicate that for many of your customers, you will simply not be important to them, so don't waste major brainpower on them. Concentrate your resources where they can do the most good. With some customers, there is the opportunity to collaborate, to take cost out of the chain, and to formulate value/cost-evaluation metrics. You as a supplier need to understand which approaches are appropriate to which customers, segment your approaches accordingly, and go more aggressively after the potential winners.

Some key changes in sales

It is important for your marketing/sales organization to identify the segment in which each customer is putting your company, and their operating approach to dealing with you. It is even more important for you to help the rest of your organization understand the segments—and to know when things might be changed, and when the best bet is just to live with the situation, with minimal investments. "One size fits all" is not the right answer. Finally, a cowardly approach to the marketplace is not the answer either. We have seen many suppliers that understand how significant improvements can be achieved by their customers, but do not push these ideas. In many cases the reason is past experience in doing so, and finding their ideas not well received. But this must not be a reason to give up totally. There should be a few customers that see their own need to transform, with the right attitude, where you can develop a plan for getting beyond the rottweilers, and where your senior managers can engage with theirs—to move away from zero-sum games.

✔ Sales today is not for the faint-hearted.

The sales organization must be proactive in its approach to different customers, finding the right approach and solution for each of them. More importantly, sales needs to identify those customers and segmentations that you might be able to change—and help determine how to change them. Finally, sales needs to have the leadership necessary to focus the organization to be able to successfully gain the business in the differing segments.

The "opportunities"

A few years ago, while working as consultants for a major food additive and flavor company, we came across an unusual (to us) situation. The company had formulated a new additive that had superior features for customers and was less expensive and more profitable to sell, but the salespeople refused to introduce it to customers. Their explanation was "Don't rock the boat—we continue to sell the existing product and do not want the customer to think about any changes."

Unilever's frozen food division was unable to sell Italian frozen spinach in a neighboring country; the explanation was, "Germans will eat only German spinach." Indeed, new frozen food products developed in one country (such as some new kind of pizza) are usually "failures" in other countries, blamed on "different tastes." A skeptic has wondered whether the real issue is a new foreign product taking the shelf space of an existing product made in the home country.

Why do French mothers happily feed their children prepared baby-food products until the age of 4 or 5, while in other European countries the marketing folks can convince mothers to use these products only until their children are 18 months old?

Does your company accept these kinds of arguments? Are your salespeople helping key customers to enhance *their* competitiveness—other than by cutting prices? Do they talk only to purchasing agents (rottweilers)? Many times there is no choice, but you need to *push* on this. Your salespeople should identify the rottweilers and systematically find ways to move out of this bind. Your company must develop more collaborative relationships and fewer combative ones than your competitors. Are your salespeople helping key customers provide new bundles of goods and services? Are they helping them move up their value chains? Are your sales/marketing folks a bunch of cowards? Do your senior managers help get around the customer rottweilers?

✔ Are you headed toward the commodity business?

Consider one company that needed a push. ICI Explosives sold explosives by the kilo to quarrying companies. This was a cut-throat business, with several competitors skimming the most profitable items while ICI offered a full line of products, backed up with extensive (mostly free) services. By developing a "mobile manufacturing unit," ICI could deliver explosives that were not dangerous until placed in the blasting holes of the rock face. Furthermore, the mobile units, in conjunction with computer modeling of the quarry, could deliver "designer rocks"—rocks blasted to reasonably tight tolerances that required much less subsequent crushing and processing.

ICI's offering represented a real step forward, but capitalizing on it required breaking out of existing sales approaches. Classic sales approaches to the customer rottweilers were not going to do it. ICI needed to identify the one or two customers who could think broadly enough to understand the potential gain in value/cost—and convince them. And it was critical to drive the internal changes needed in ICI to support this new customer segment. Senior managers needed to augment existing practices to change the game in both ICI and in the key customer companies.

Key sales elements

Today's aggressive procurement practices require a strong, coordinated response from your sales organization. The changes need to be well thought out and embedded in key strategic choices:

✔ As a supplier, you need to select the key customers.

Deploy the right resources

For those that are not pure rottweilers—or see the internal need to move selectively beyond this approach—you must determine carefully what you could provide that changes the game, figure out who to sell to in the customer's organization, design the selling package, be clear about what customers will require, and then—most importantly—be ready to deploy the resources throughout *your* company to deliver the promise. This is a change process that goes way beyond sales.

The change process also includes the changes required on the customer side. In the case of ICI Explosives, the "sell" needed to include the changes necessary in the customer company—new ordering/contracting, outsourcing of blasting to ICI, etc.

Establishing collaborative relationships is a tough job. The good news is that salespeople are probably better able to do so than purchasing people. They have incentives that support dramatic increases in volume, supporting customers is integrated into internal thinking, and most firms see sales as more "sexy" than purchasing.

In Chapter 1, we showed that in the Skanska–Rockwool partnership Rockwool was better able to leverage the learning. It sold Skanska a much-expanded business relationship based on working with Rockwool's Finnish parent, Partek. More interestingly, once the cost reduction potential was clear, Rockwool sold the collaboration package to other key actors, including Sweden's largest players in the do-it-yourself business. To these chain store operators, Rockwool, with other key suppliers and the third-party logistics operator, could offer a significant cost reduction potential—although again, this required major changes by the customer as well. Rockwool thereafter segmented its sales approach to match its different potential customers.

Clearly identify the potential

Selling collaboration requires a well thought-out approach to: "Where's the beef?" The obvious answers for ICI customers are lower total costs, easier operations, and reduced risk from explosive materials being misused. For Rockwool customers, they are combined logistics with significantly reduced costs, more effective information systems, and reduced inventories/stock-outs. But if the ICI customer contacts are limited to purchasing people who are exclusively evaluated on the basis of the price per kilo of explosive, the game is over. Similarly, Rockwool also needed to break out of classic selling for the key customers.

More generally, the potential payoffs include sharply reduced non-recurring costs such as contracting, reduction/elimination of many transactions such as ordering, streamlining of sales/ordering with personnel reductions, standardization/modularity with reduced numbers of items, joint design, and increased speed—in all activities.

Let's take an overview of where hard unit cost payoffs can come from in a true collaborative effort. If you were to examine your company's cost structure, it might not look too different from the following simplified example:

- Annual sales = $3 million
- Plant and equipment = $1 million (annual depreciation = $100,000)
- Cost of materials = 60 percent of sales ($1.8 million)
- Cost of labor = 20 percent ($600,000)
- Variable overhead cost = 5 percent ($150,000)
- Fixed overhead = 5 percent ($150,000)
- Profit before tax = $200,000 (6.7 percent).

Let us assume this company operates one weekly 40-hour shift. If it operates two shifts (and the simplified cost structure holds), the profits go up to $650,000 (10.8 percent). But the profit on the incremental business is $450,000 (15 percent). The numbers are, as expected, even more dramatic for three-shift operation (12.2 percent). More importantly, if this company is willing to forgo a portion of the incremental profit in reduced prices on the incremental business, the results are equally stunning: If for three-shift operations profits were to double from $200,000 to $400,000, prices could be reduced on the incremental volume by 11.6 percent.

You might argue with the cost accounting here, but the overall point is clear: If you can fill your factory, you can afford to engage in very aggressive pricing. This now becomes the task of your best salespeople: To find customers that can fill up the capacity in creative ways that do not disrupt "regular" business. This is, in fact, a demonstration of how the super-supplier concept works.

> ✔ But these must be delivered, and low-balling the changes needed in both firms is not a good idea.

Underestimating the change agenda in both firms—individually and jointly—will lead to disappointing results, difficulty in sustaining the efforts, and poor perceptions on both sides. Insisting that you will run at full capacity doesn't mean you will—or even that you can.

Pick smart customers

As noted in Chapter 1, we strongly warn you not to ally yourself with stupid partners. In picking smart customers, the key questions are:

- Is this company a leader in its industry?
- Is it a key source for learning?
- Are its internal practices state-of-the-art?
- Does it actively share its knowledge with key suppliers and their customers to develop joint competencies?

Every supplier makes comparisons of its customers, ranging from off-the-cuff opinions to systematic benchmarking. In the latter case, a smart supplier will know how well each of its customers is doing in its marketplace and the basis for the customer's ability to compete:

- How good are the products?
- How sharp is the company's R&D?
- Time to market?
- How fast does it adapt to change?
- What are the attitudes and approach in procurement—rottweiler or partner?
- How good are its operations—world-class or sloppy?
- How good is its planning system—extent of changes?
- What are its improvement programs—and progress achieved?
- Is the improvement focus solely internal, on pushing the suppliers, or joint?
- Who are its supplier and customer partners—and *their* reputations?
- How open is the company to new ideas?

So how do suppliers form these opinions? Is there more to it than perceptions, and asking your salespeople? Many of the key issues can be addressed through standard benchmarking approaches, and you should always visit customer factories.

A visit to the Tetra Pak factory in Singapore is illustrative. The plant's most important equipment is its multicolor printing presses, and the key operational issue with them is to increase the percentage of time they are making good products. Tetra Pak measures "overall equipment effectiveness," which sets 24/7 operation as a standard and lowers performance for not running all shifts, not running at full speed, changeovers, poor quality, etc. Tetra Pak adopted this metric some years ago and continually drives improvements in it. These include major reductions in changeover times, standardization of inks, and even buying all of the company's paper from a single supplier—in Sweden, of all places. It turns out that the extra shipping costs and higher purchase price are more than made up by the paper's near-perfect uniformity, which permits faster changeovers, lower scrap in roll changes, and sharply reduced adjustment times. Tetra Pak clearly qualifies as a smart customer, one that will pay for new ideas, not just look for price reductions.

✔ The same set of issues applies to examining whether your *suppliers* are smart.

It is amazing to see how many companies are asking their suppliers for open books, which is largely an exercise in advanced rottweiler training. What is much more useful is "open factories," since if your suppliers are inefficient, you are paying for it. The issues illustrated in the Tetra Pak example apply here as well. Visit the supplier's factories:

- How many expensive pieces of equipment are idle?
- What is the supplier doing in terms of lean manufacturing/operational excellence?
- How does it stack up relative to its competitors?
- If there are idle facilities, and this is due to a shortage of orders, what can you do to fix the situation?

As one final note on this theme, you need to take a hard look at your own operations. What would be the measure of "overall equipment effectiveness" in *your* factory? Are you expecting your customers to pay for your inefficiency? Are you demanding your suppliers to subsidize your poor operations? What do you need to do to improve capacity utilization? How much might this be worth?

Overcome the country disease

The "country disease" is often found in multinational firms that evaluate their operations in national silos. It is prevalent in both customers and suppliers. It can block many efforts in collaboration. Consider Unilever's French ice-cream division, which once regarded its UK sister company—rather than Nestlé—as its biggest competitor. This was overcome only when country manager bonuses became more based on divisional results, and when different countries' management teams spent time together in education sessions. As a supplier to Unilever ice-cream, it was virtually impossible to achieve the potential payoffs we have enumerated when it suffered from the country disease. As a customer to Unilever ice-cream, improvements were equally unlikely when all ice-cream came uniquely from one country source.

It is important to understand the impact of the country disease both as a supplier and as a customer. If your operation suffers from this malady, it will be impossible to deliver a whole host of potential advantages to your customers. As a customer, if this is your problem, no supplier partnership can deliver the significant payoffs from standardization of products and processes. In today's increasingly global competition, most large firms recognize the need to act more holistically—to reduce the country disease. But as a supplier, you need to understand the implications in a customer making these changes, such as volume concentration, standardization, common processes, transaction simplification, and supply chain rationalization. Are you going to help? Act proactively? Or sit and wait?

If either your key suppliers or your key customers suffer from the country disease, their ability to gain major competitive advantage is sharply limited. An assessment of the country disease must be made before undertaking a significant collaborative relationship. It is far too easy to see the potential benefits without realizing the painful transformation that must accompany their achievement.

In 2004, Numico recruited for its global purchasing team in Amsterdam a talented Chinese woman for the company's portfolio of amino acids. The major Numico production unit using these ingredients was located in Liverpool. There was considerable price pressure being applied to the end products, and Numico needed to find a lower-cost supply. Doing so was only half of the game. The local purchasing manager had held his position for 35 years and relied on a well-established local supplier base. It took considerable diplomacy, including regular early morning easyJet flights to Liverpool, active listening, an understanding attitude of the local challenges, and even CEO involvement to create the internal changes needed. After about two years of hard work, Numico's new supplier is Asian, resulting in structurally more cost-effective factories. Moreover, as a new entrant in the market, the supplier has been keen to go the extra mile and provide consignment stock, extended payment terms, and quality guarantees. In return, for the first time Numico signed a multiyear contract with an "exotic" supplier for a strategic ingredient.

Sell the ideas—internally *and to the customer*. Developing a collaborative relationship—and evolving it into a working partnership—requires significant selling internally and to the collaborative partner. Moreover, sometimes it simply cannot work.

> ✔ You can't change dogs to cats, and it is sometimes equally difficult to change rottweilers to collaborative procurement persons.

The real message here is that establishing collaborative relationships represents a significant change in both strategy and practices. Both customer and supplier must see a genuine win–win. Without a clear commitment at the top of both companies, the chances of success are severely limited. Collaboration requires a leap of faith.

We need trust. As noted in the example of Hewlett-Packard and Canon, there is an unwritten law at HP: if you screw up the company's relationship with Canon, you're fired. Selecting the right targets for collaboration requires a subsequent commitment and continuing education and unlearning: What do you need to do—and not do—to make this collaboration truly effective? What actions should you take in the best interest of the collaboration, even when they hurt immediate results at your business unit or firm? How do you keep the faith and support your partner?

Although it is hard to instill collaborative efforts in a firm, it is doubly difficult to instill them in a *pair* of firms. Experience indicates that periodic face-to-face contacts—say, drinking beer at a neutral bar—are essential for this to become a reality. It is just too easy to fall back to zero-sum thinking or to cut a corner for an immediate gain on your side. When one of us asked the key contact at Caterpillar how the partnership with ABB had been facilitated, he immediately answered: "red wine."

Deploying your sales resources

Collaborative relationships are appropriate and possible for only a subset of customers, and partnerships for a smaller subset of these, with pair of aces relationships limited by the "magic ten" restriction. You need to make clear choices, and you must deploy your smartest salespeople to go after these choices. The faint at heart will not deliver the desired results.

This implies choice, and as was true for choosing suppliers, you need to be careful. This is more than just selecting the big customers. Some customers are just not important—and never will be. For others, you as a supplier may never seem important. But do not be too quick about these conclusions.

The Bossard Group, located in Zug, Switzerland, sells the most mundane of products: nuts, screws, and other kinds of fasteners. Who would wish to partner with this firm? Surely customers would buy such commodities through reverse auctions or let individual units buy locally? But Bossard can demonstrate nicely that the fasteners themselves account for only 15 percent of a customer's total cost; the other 85 percent comes from ordering, inventory holding, logistics, and assorted transactions. Further, there is a notable lack of standardization in fasteners, which leads to many extra costs in inventory, storage, and obsolescence. Bossard can take over the whole works: all orders, replenishments, minimal transactions, simple two-bin systems, product rationalization, and quality certifications—all on a global basis—including supporting shifts in production to lower-cost countries.

✔ You should not base the computation on the unit price of fasteners.

There are two morals to this story. First, there is a need to truly understand the business of some customers—they may not even be seen as key customers initially. But could you provide a solution to a problem—one that they may not even know they have? Second, is how to sell it—even if you can prove decisively, from a TCO perspective, that the customer will save significant sums of money? Again, selling this solution requires going around the rottweilers. Your salespeople will need to sell a different bundle of goods and services—at a different level.

Let us now consider a somewhat different kind of "opportunity." A few years ago, Nestlé initiated Project Globe, the company's plan to meet the challenge of global demand from the big retailers. Wal-Mart and Carrefour are asking for uniform worldwide pricing, with greatly simplified ordering, logistics, and other transactions. For Nestlé, this requires a massive change process to integrate the efforts of all factories and supply chains, in all geographic regions, with a common set of processes and information systems. But the first objective was one of efficiency: Nestlé wished to reduce its annual sales and administrative overhead expenses by 4.7 percent of sales (roughly $3 billion). Project Globe was initially budgeted for five years and a cost of $2.4 billion, about half of annual profits. This is a huge project, and Nestlé senior managers continually insist that it is not an information systems project. In fact, it provides the basis for rationalization of the supply chain—major product standardization and serious consolidation of the supplier base.

✔ What does this mean if you are a Nestlé supplier?

A good guess is that Nestlé will reduce the number of its suppliers by something like 75 percent, with those remaining having much greater volumes. But these suppliers will need to support Nestlé on a global/regional basis, with greatly simplified ways of working and lower costs. Playing this game will require massive changes to be implemented. Waiting for Nestlé to invite you to participate is not a brilliant idea; in this case, salespeople need to do a lot more than selling. Nestlé is already convinced that collaborative ideas are the way to go—the key question is whether *your firm* can execute them.

Being the most attractive supplier

In Chapter 2, we discussed how a customer needs to be attractive to its suppliers. The most attractive customer will be able to attract the best suppliers—those who will devote their brainpower to solving the customer's problems, happily engaging in joint projects to improve value/cost.

The same set of ideas applies to suppliers—you need to be seen as the most attractive supplier to your customers. And again, this must not be done by shaving your margins down to nothing.

✔ You need to be attractive as a supplier, but you deserve to be paid for it.

Flawless execution: the ante to play the game

In order to be seen as an attractive supplier, you must have flawless execution. Deliveries must be on time, quality must approach perfection, problems must be minimal, and responses to unforeseen conditions must be swift. Moreover, prices must be competitive. Without these conditions, there is no possibility of establishing collaborative relationships that can be grown into more fundamental forms of cooperation.

Flawless execution is not a one-time event but, rather, an ongoing, ever-present imperative. Furthermore, the expectations for flawless execution continually evolve. As a collaborative relationship develops further, the complexity of joint operations also increases.

In Chapter 3, we discussed the "tough love" approach, and why a customer should always drive for lower costs and continuous improvement. This is equally applicable to the supplier side. You as a supplier must also always push the envelope, but the real payoffs are found in joint efforts to improve value/cost. Flawless execution remains the underlying prerequisite.

What makes a supplier attractive?

As we noted in Chapter 3, many customer companies express a desire for their key suppliers to be innovators, but those suppliers often complain that their suggestions go unheard. Since purchasing personnel are continually pushed in their organizations to reduce prices, suppliers that can do so are naturally viewed as attractive. The flipside is also true: A well-known large supplier of packaging has a unique packaging solution—it sets standard prices and refuses to negotiate. Perhaps not surprisingly, this supplier is often rated as highly unattractive. But the plain truth is that this packaging supplier has a superior product; we have seen examples where alternatives have been substituted, but they were in fact less effective.

There is a fundamental difference between price reductions based on negotiating muscle and those based on joint efforts by the pair of aces to engineer costs out of the supply chain. The suppliers that are ready to engage in these joint cost-reduction efforts should be seen as attractive, but this cannot be one-sided: The customer must also invest time and energy in changing the inter-company processes.

Committing to the future—together

In Chapter 1, we described the "super-supplier" as one form of a pair of aces. It is useful to here understand how the relationship between Honda of America and its sheet metal supplier had to grow over a significant time period. There were many chances for it to go off the track, and there were inevitable hiccups along the way. In every case, there was a need to deal with the issues, sort out any short-term problems, get flawless execution back on track, and not lose the faith. The evolution—from arm's length, buyer–supplier relationship, to one of collaboration, to one of partnership, to one of pair of aces—requires a strong commitment along every step of the way.

Honda's goals during this evolution also shifted. The initial focus was on efficiency, as the engine driving down the unit cost. But at some point, it became essential to find ways to maximize capacity utilization while respecting the auto maker's delivery schedules. It is *joint* problem identification and solutions that must drive this relationship—forever focused on improvement. And at some point, the goals have to shift: Unit cost becomes a basic requirement (part of "flawless execution"), and the game shifts to joint work on the combined cash flow, speed, innovation, and new product development.

Ten golden rules for being an attractive supplier

It is critical to see how each of these rules impacts the sales and marketing organization: many are their direct responsibility, but several are not and therefore need to be sold to others in the company:

1. **Execute flawlessly.** This is the ante to play cooperative games. Without it, there is no point in trying.
2. **Tell the truth.** Do not hide problems that influence the customer. It is better to hear them from you formally—early—than informally later.
3. **Select/choose/segment.** Don't try to be super-attractive to all your customers. You need to develop skills that can be leveraged for the long run.
4. **Don't flog dead horses.** Some customers are disingenuous and will use a supplier initiative only to hammer on prices. Trust must be real.

5. **Encourage selected customers to be interested in more than prices.** For instance, innovation/speed/responsiveness/flexibility. But if these deliver extra value, they deserve higher prices.

6. **Work to create joint metrics, then work to kill off those that are wrong.** Track the metrics as a key assessment of the relationship. It is essential to always get better and not rest on your laurels.

7. **Create awareness in your company of special customer relationships.** Why they are important, and the benefits you are gaining from them.

8. **Be very open about intellectual property issues.** Confidentiality and exclusivity must be transparent. No surprises here.

9. **Expect misalignment.** Manage it, and develop escalation processes. Don't expect "no problems." Try to anticipate them.

10. **Be ready to accept all challenges.** Respond to customer demands to help with its marketplace pressures—as long as these demands are not unilateral: We will always work with you.

Delivering what customers *need*

Each of your critical customers has unique needs and unique processes/ways of working. The better you understand them, the better you can deliver the right bundle of goods and services—and be compensated accordingly.

Making key account management a reality

Your company team needs to help key customers move up their value chains when this provides them a competitive advantage. What are the order-winning bundles of goods and services for them? How might you help them provide/deliver these bundles? What are the necessary joint changes required to make this a reality? In most cases, the breakthrough payoffs necessitate some new ways for you as a supplier to interact with these key customers. It is collaborative—and more. New infrastructure and ways of operating are required: new procurement processes, new sales processes, joint planning, transaction simplification, and new metrics.

ABB has five major divisions, based on the products provided: Power Products (e.g. transformers and voltage switchgear), Power Systems (e.g. turnkey power-distribution grids), Automation Products (e.g. motors and low-voltage products), Process Automation (e.g. integrated process-control systems), and Robotics (e.g.

industrial robots and robotic systems). But many of ABB's major customers are the same for each of the product divisions. Sending different salespeople to the same customer is not always the best idea. ABB has, as noted, developed KAMs for these customers. The KAMs can better identify the true needs of a customer, particularly when those needs are for a large project.

The project starts with the customer's real needs, then identifies the portions of the project that can be provided by ABB's product-oriented division. The project might also call for items not produced by ABB. Finally, the project is like a systems solution. The project is more than the sum of its component parts; integration of those parts and a timely delivery/ramp-up are a key deliverable. The opportunity for ABB is to help the customer bring the project online and ramp it up: with no problems, with better results, in a shorter time span. All of this implies major payoffs for the customer, especially in terms of improving cash flow. Doing so allows ABB to capture a larger percentage of the project budget, gaining added business for several of its product divisions, perhaps plus fees for managing the project.

So this looks like a clear win–win. But saying it is so doesn't make it so. In fact, delivering the promise here mandates major change requirements for ABB, and for each of its divisions, as well as for its key customers. The KAM concept sounds like a no-brainer choice. But this assumes the customer is oriented—and organized—accordingly. If the customer does purchasing based on commodities, there may not be an opportunity to sell "solutions."

On the ABB side, selling/delivering solutions requires coordinating the sale/delivery across product divisions, as well as some overriding form of project management. As the number of customers who are treated as key accounts grows—in a linear way—the complexity of fitting this into the various product division and business unit structures increases geometrically.

Taking on complexity

The key account management issues are only one example of the more general problem of how to sell/deliver what key customers need. You need to develop the competencies necessary to take on the customer's problems—and deliver integrated systems solutions. It well may be that you will also need to help the customer to overcome problems at its end. For example, if a customer has the "country disease," a key part of the improvement agenda will be curing the ailment. You might be able to help the customer along the way, creating a very different definition of value/cost in this relationship.

Similarly, you should probably investigate the extent of standardization that your customers have in their products, services, and processes. There well may be large opportunities here. But it is important not to underestimate the accompanying challenges. Remember the Chapter 3 example of Unilever and the Magnum ice-cream bar wrappers. If you—as a supplier and collaborative partner—understand the journey well, you should be able to help your customer through the transition.

It is important for you—as a preferred supplier—to understand your key customers' problems and challenges. In doing so, it will be useful to know which approaches you have developed that might be modified and used again. It is also important to gather the learning from other examples. To the extent that your company can proactively help key customers solve their problems—with you removing complexity from their lives—you can develop win–win situations and long-term customer loyalty.

So how many of these key account management teams can you mount simultaneously? Our rule of ten is probably a good start, although at some point the new ways of working should become routine. Then, more teams might be deployed.

Measuring the right things

No one will disagree with this statement, but the key question is, what *are* the right things? Which ones are wrong? If you and your key customers are to jointly transform the bundles of goods and services you provide, it is critical to establish metrics that indicate when the transformation is going well and vice versa. For the ABB example, one clear set of measures would focus on time and flawless execution: Is ABB delivering the various pieces of the project bundle as agreed? Is the project on schedule, and if not, why not? What is needed to recover? When do we know there is trouble? How do we make sure that problems are not hidden? How do we respond to new requirements not foreseen at the outset? How can ABB and the customer act like a true partnership? All problems are *our* problems—not *mine* and *yours*.

Measures that focus only on concrete performance are not enough. Once again, we strongly recommend use of perception-based metrics to see how various individuals *feel* about the ways the two firms are working together. It is useful to periodically ask many people in both companies their opinions (something like a five-point scale) on topics such as:

- Is this joint effort a win–win?
- Is our partner sharing the rewards?
- Is our partner holding up its end in the joint work?
- Does our partner do its homework?
- Can we depend on its people?
- Does it make decisions expeditiously—and stick by them?
- Can we trust our partner?
- Do we share common objectives?

Making these assessments on a periodic basis allows you to develop a time series, to assess alignment inside each firm—and jointly. Further, problems can be seen before they get out of hand—and before they result in poor results in the concrete measures. That is, the perception-based measures are a leading indicator; concrete measures will lag.

Finally, you need to understand that neither you nor your key customer ever will truly know what each other *needs*—you must jointly figure it out as you go. In fact, whenever you think you know, you must jointly step back and see how you can augment the "needs."

✔ A partnership is not a partnership without an ongoing shared-improvement agenda.

So what?

Implementing collaboration from the customer side needs to be seen as essentially identical to doing so from the supplier side. Smart procurement and smart sales are two sides of the same coin, where the gold is finding and developing the key relationships—eventually into pairs of aces. The power of two means smart buying *and* smart selling! This is the long-run best bet for gaining and keeping your competitive advantage.

Sales cowards will need to be replaced. Maybe some can make the transition, but do not be overly optimistic. Selling what the customers really need requires breaking out of standard ways of approaching the customers. It takes guts and determination.

More importantly, this cannot be accomplished by "lone rangers."

- Your company will need to make some strategic decisions, such as the ABB commitment to key account management.
- You will need to make key choices. With which customers can you develop collaborative relationships?
- You will need to develop project teams and effective project management to deliver the promise.
- You will need to unlearn many ideas—ways of selling and buying—in your company as well as in the customer's.
- You will need to jointly develop new systems and processes.
- You will need new measures to evaluate progress and those who deliver it.

Chapter 5 ends our three chapters describing the benefits from changing the ways you buy and sell. None of this is easy, but the benefits are huge and the transformation is possible. We now turn to how this can be done.

Developing pairs of aces

Back in 1981, Harvard Business School Professor C. Wickham Skinner wrote an article in the *Harvard Business Review* lamenting the great gap between theory and practice in human resource management. It was entitled "Big hat, no cattle." In the previous five chapters, we have outlined the payoffs from the power of two: customer–supplier collaboration, resulting in selected pairs of aces. It is now time to deliver the bacon—to switch from "what" to "how." So do we have more than a big hat?

Bombardier Transport is a good example. It has recently developed close cooperation with ten suppliers, and these relationships are continually being improved, with some important benefits. At this point, it may be too early to brand these as pairs of aces, but one or two seem headed in this direction. BT is also working on developing a second group of collaborative supplier relationships. We see some key lessons learnt from all of this, as well as from the experiences of some other firms—in developing collaboration, but more importantly, in nurturing it to achieve breakthrough results.

Success is easily killed

It is fairly easy to convince people of the payoffs from collaboration. Making it a reality is a different story, requiring "unlearning" of many common business approaches. But even that is not enough— you need to understand the land mines and how to avoid them.

Why do customer–supplier "marriages" often end in divorce?

We know who your worst supplier is: a sister company. Worst customers also tend to be sisters. Why? Fundamentally, inter-company relationships have a tendency to become complacent: The "contract" is secure, and no one is seriously pushing for major improvements. The same danger of complacency exists in any customer–supplier collaborative relationship, and grows as the relationship deepens and switching costs increase.

One interesting indicator of customer–supplier complacency in many firms is a reliance on traditional definitions of "customer satisfaction."

- ✔ One study of airline ontime departure performance found the winner to be Ethiopian Airlines. It kept changing the departure times until the planes left.

- ✔ Still another study was of social justice, where the expectation was that lower rates of protest would indicate high levels of social justice. The winner was Communist Bulgaria, followed by North Korea.

We have encountered suppliers who tell us they have 99 percent ontime delivery, but their performance measures resemble those of Ethiopian Airlines. The customer measures are rarely the same as those of the supplier.

In fact, customer satisfaction includes a lot more than ontime delivery. If this is your measure of customer service, you are almost certainly getting it wrong. Typical improvements in assessing customer satisfaction are to add service and product-quality metrics, but these require agreement as to what will be measured—how and by whom?

In customer–supplier collaborative relationships, delivery and quality are part of "flawless execution," which is the ante to play the game. What become more important are issues of trust, communications, and joint commitment by the parties. And, as noted in Chapter 4, it is the *perceptions* of these things that are the drivers—classic measures are passengers at best.

What this means in practice is that it is far too easy as a supplier to keep internal measures of ontime delivery and quality that make you believe that all is well with a key customer. And again, these "feel good" assessments might be quite different at the customer end. But even if they are basically the same, there is still a good possibility that complacency has settled into the relationship. Other issues will almost certainly be more important for key people in the customer company.

An equally complacent misreading can occur from the customer's side. In fact, our experience is that customers are much more myopic than suppliers. They tend to think:

- We are a good customer, and our suppliers all love us.
- We are easy to do business with.
- Whenever there are problems, it is the suppliers' fault.
- We give them all the information they need.

In fact, as we've stated, no customer–supplier partnership is truly a partnership unless it has a significant improvement agenda. This is not a one-sided set of demands—it must be a joint agenda, with improvement work for both parties and a clear win–win articulated. It also must have open communication in which all faults and potential improvements are considered gold nuggets to be mined. In the absence of these imperatives, the customer–supplier marriage is very likely headed for complacency and, ultimately, divorce.

A tale of woe

A few years ago, we wrote a case study of two firms (we called the customer Freqon and the supplier NordAlu). The case is especially interesting because it examined the two companies' relationship over a 12-year period. During this span, it was possible to assess the relationship in terms of joint learning/competency development, networking and informal relationships, joint improvement projects undertaken, and the sales volume between the two companies. Figure 6.1 (overleaf) provides a time series of these concepts.

As can be seen, the projects, networking, and joint learning are the leading indicators, with sales the lagging indicator. By the time the sales start to drop in year ten, there is no longer any significant joint activity between the two firms.

Underlying this figure are the various actions that created these results. In short, over time Freqon shifted procurement with

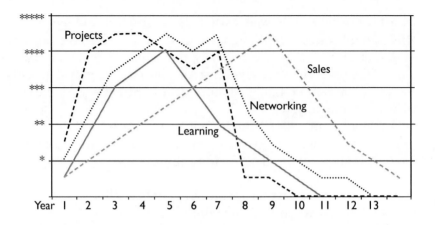

Figure 6.1 Leading and lagging indicators

NordAlu from the engineering group to professional purchasing (rottweilers). A different cast of characters came into the relationship on both sides. Key people moved on; old friendships were forgotten. NordAlu did not hold up its end in driving cost out of the product, and NordAlu found a new customer that was more cooperative.

The bottom line to this story is that this was a very good collaborative relationship that deteriorated. They did significant joint work, it was most useful in supporting new product development, and it should have been improved to enable the customer to reduce costs in line with market needs; but the relationship became complacent, and cost reduction was not attempted on a collaborative basis. It ended with minimal sales and an arm's-length association.

Maintaining obsolete ideas

It is useful to push the "marriage" metaphor to see the need for more informed thinking to support collaboration, as well as to to understand the need for different language. Classic purchasing is laced with ideas and their associated vocabulary that are the antithesis of collaboration:

• Would you "evaluate" your spouse?

- Do you "measure" your spouse?
- Do you assess his or her value?
- Do you "manage" him or her?
- Do you select a spouse through competitive bidding?
- Do you rate him or her with some scorecard?
- Do you hide information?
- Do you have a zero-sum approach?

We believe that sustaining success requires a different vocabulary and associated ways of thinking. The better terms for fostering a customer–supplier collaborative relationship are words such as build, share, nurture, entrust, empower, sustain, shared values, alignment, joint vision, and enhancement.

Constant danger

Collaboration is in constant danger of being ruined. It is like some tool that accumulates rust—it must be continually polished and sharpened. All it takes is for one person to initiate some one-sided action to significantly damage trust, the cornerstone of collaboration. Doing so has to be explicitly forbidden:

✔ Leadership here must exhibit self-discipline and trust, so that collaboration becomes widely accepted and the norm.

Keeping the faith

We started this chapter by talking about killing off collaborative success instead of growing it, because the danger is high and the chances are good for collaboration to go astray. Let us now turn to some remedies against complacency and deteriorating partnership relationships.

Making nurture explicit

The idea that a collaborative relationship will stay fine—without active efforts to keep it that way—is at best amazingly naïve. furthermore, as Figure 6.1 clearly shows, good results follow from joint efforts. If the relationship lacks a significant improvement agenda, it will almost surely become complacent.

✔ "Standing still" is an illusion; "moving forward" is a
   necessity.

Companies with successful collaborative relationships often establish some form of ombudsman. It is even better when both companies in the relationship have ombudsmen. The goal is to have an
explicit activity to be triggered at an early stage when things go
awry. The operating assumption is that things *will* go awry—it is
just unclear when and where. By finding—and treating—misalignment problems early, damage to the relationship can be more than
minimized. There is a good chance that early, proactive problem
resolution can enhance the feeling of cooperation. We have noted
that ABB and Caterpillar have established an explicit "governance
process," which includes regular meetings where the focus is less
on detailed problems and more on processes and what needs to be
done next.

Nurture and continuous improvement require a set of measures
that support these goals. Getting better needs to be demonstrated
concretely; win–win means that the improvements will be valued by
both customer and supplier; achieving these results will come from
only joint efforts rather than unilateral demands. More importantly,
following the logic of Figure 6.1, successful joint efforts should lead,
in a "virtuous circle," to further nurture and ongoing win–win.

Getting better comes in two varieties: ongoing small steps and big
leaps. Both are necessary. The latter require some "godfathering" at
a high level in both companies, since major changes are usually
required in the way key individuals interact. Godfathering also
makes sense because the number of big leaps needs to be kept in
bounds and explicitly identified. Big-leap choices should be carefully
chosen and seen for what they are; taking risks is fine, but not
knowing they are being taken is not. Chapter 2 described four stages
of collaboration: Each is a big leap with successive stages requiring
major changes in the ways of thinking as well as the ways of
working.

Measuring nurture and improvement

Measures of improvement need to be periodic, they need to track
progress, and they need to be meaningful to those most affected by
them. If the time between assessments is long, it is harder to make

small corrections. An ongoing time series allows you to assess progress and to see short-term deviations. Visible win–win progress fosters ongoing commitment to joint efforts. And those who must take on the hard work in joint efforts need to see that their success is being measured and appreciated. When the joint efforts are toward breakthrough change, it is important that the measures demonstrate the results.

We are strong believers in perception-based metrics: In the end, it is what people *think* is correct or true that will drive their actions. Perceptions also have the virtue of relativity. Something may look OK in terms of some static metric, but relative to other activities it might not stack up so well. If your firm does indeed have something like ten pair of aces relationships, these must be continually perceived as most important, as receiving the best deployment of people and other assets, and as being improved at the fastest pace relative to others.

The perception-based metrics for each collaborative relationship perhaps should be selected based on the particular issues involved, but in general there are several key issues. We see periodic evaluation of each of these—in both customer and supplier (perhaps with some minor language change)—where those asked for opinions are the people most impacted by the relationship and most actively involved in it, either managing the relationship or making the improvements. The perceptions could include:

- flawless execution (delivery and quality)
- trust/shared vision
- commitment by the other side
- communication/openness
- progress on improvements/projects
- quality of the "glue" between the firms.

We have one final set of ideas on continuous improvement, nurture, and pushing the collaborative efforts. It is important to benchmark, to compare with the best ideas—those that break out of existing ways of working. These can be inside the company but often are outside. You can learn a great deal from sharing practice, particularly with mavericks. It is also important for your company to establish good role models: What kinds of behavior are most likely to lead to significant results? How much of this is based on technical expertise versus good networking/communication skills? How is individual performance being measured and rewarded?

Negotiation II

The "how" of collaboration must include a redefinition of negotiation. We call the new game "Negotiation II" to differentiate it from the traditional way. Classic approaches may be useful for short-term price negotiations in which zero-sum thinking is the rule of the day, but win–win basically rules out this kind of behavior. Does this imply an end to negotiation? Of course not. But negotiation will significantly change in focus and form. Making this statement must be followed up by concrete actions. Far too many firms talk partnerships and collaboration while behaving out of pure self-interest. A prospective partner needs to clearly determine: Is this real collaboration or disguised rottweiler behavior?

We recently worked with a company that awarded contracts to a supplier but continued to negotiate with its competitors as if the deal had not been signed. This was for two purposes: To keep the other suppliers feeling that they were still in the game, and to keep the winning supplier competitive. Any lower bid would be used to "further negotiate"—or even change suppliers at the last minute. Needless to say, the level of trust on the part of the suppliers was low.

The key here is to recognize that the negotiation leopard needs to change its spots. The objective is still cost reduction, but the means to that end must change. Instead of the two firms expending energy in playing rottweiler-based games, the efforts now are placed where they can do more good: in engineering cost out of the product through new design, better scheduling and coordination, more effective use of the supplier's capacity, reduction of transaction costs, and increased speed.

More fundamentally, the joint efforts need to push beyond the classic definitions of work for the customer and supplier. Where each firm will be positioned in the value chain is the key here. Figure 6.2 shows the concept. Joint efforts need to focus on who can do

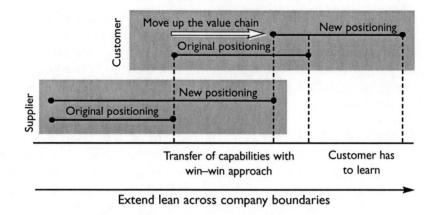

Figure 6.2 Changing customer and supplier positioning

what best, where each company should be positioned in the value chain, and how the concept of "lean" needs to be extended from a single company focus to one of lean for a collaborative partnership.

Negotiation II needs to reflect a fundamental shift in belief. The goal for both parties in a collaborative relationship must be the same:

✔ We want to manage preferential treatment.

As a customer, we wish for—no, we *demand*—preferential treatment from our key suppliers. But we will not achieve it by deploying rottweilers. We are going to achieve preferential treatment because we are this supplier's most attractive customer, and it is in the supplier's best interests to give us this treatment. When it does so, it wins too, more than by working with competitors.

The same argument holds for the supplier. We demand preferential treatment from this customer. They treat us better than our competitors because we are a more attractive supplier to them. We jointly increase joint value/cost, we learn from each other, and this is the best way for our firm to develop its competitive advantage.

Tough benchmarks

For many people, collaboration sounds like soft-headed, professorial nonsense. One key to avoiding the potential complacency in collaboration is to periodically subject the partnership to the toughest benchmarks that can be found. These include low-cost country sourcing and other alternatives, but the basic processes really need to be subjected to occasional "out of the box" thinking. For example, we often expose firms to the supply chains in other companies/industries:

- Zara, the Spanish clothing manufacturer, is a good example. While other clothing companies renew their collections two or three times per year, Zara does it every two weeks; the time from new design creation to finished products is a matter of days. The feedback from what is selling to what is designed and subsequently manufactured is extremely fast. Furthermore, individual Zara stores do not order: they are sent merchandise from the central logistics operation. The merchandise is unique and will not be replaced by the same items. If a customer likes something, it is imperative to buy it—now! The net result is a much lower percentage of merchandise sold at sale prices.
- Johnson & Johnson at one time brought a team focusing on faster changeovers to watch a Formula 1 team change tires. This had been preceded by a J&J executive determining that it took less than eight hours to make a Toyota from start to finish—while J&J took something like eight weeks to make a Band-Aid.
- Then there was the Ford–Mazda comparison in the early 1980s, of the number of people working in accounts payable. At first Mazda managers did not understand the question how many, but they then counted and came up with five; Ford had 500. With JIT approaches, traditional methods are often superfluous. If Mazda finished 2,000 cars today, it undoubtedly used 2,000 radiators, so it pays the radiator manufacturer accordingly. There are so few radiators in inventory that no one cares about keeping track of them.

Bombardier Transport uses a different kind of tough benchmark. Management calls it the "wild card." Essentially, BT continually searches for an alternative supplier that is ready to deliver some key component at a significantly lower price than an existing supplier. Potential suppliers need, of course, to be evaluated to determine whether the firm can indeed deliver and make sure that this is not just a one-shot, money-losing chance to establish a relationship—

one that will later necessitate higher prices. But the wild cards, if used right, can stimulate a customer—and its key suppliers—to continually push beyond current ways of working and current process constraints.

You really need to go beyond classic metrics

There are several popular and widely advocated supply chain management measurement approaches. All focus on some important issues, but we see them as falling critically short in dealing with joint customer–supplier value/cost improvement. In essence, their focus is entirely one-sided. One of the best-known measurement schemes is the Supply Chain Operations Reference (SCOR) model, which purports to measure the end-to-end supply chain. SCOR is composed of four classic supply chain processes: plan, source, make, and deliver. These are seen as being done in each company in a supply chain. The SCOR model also includes metrics for order fulfillment, order cycle time, forecast accuracy, inventory turnover, cash-to-cash, etc. But all of these metrics are internally focused with minimal win–win emphasis.

An example that shows the bias even more clearly is seen in Figure 6.3 (overleaf), which comes from the AMR Benchmark Analytix.

As can be seen from this pyramid, the focus is on results for *our* company, not our customers or our suppliers. The suppliers are "evaluated"—there is no joint assessment, any problems in supplier delivery are assumed to be their fault, the emphasis is internal, and the improvement approach will be largely how to squeeze the lemon. At best, metric approaches such as this are necessary but insufficient. At worst, they foster zero-sum thinking, inhibit development of partnership behavior, and hinder breakthrough results.

It takes two to tango

Collaboration is a great objective, but you need to make it more tangible if at all possible. This works well when the two firms can clearly identify strategic objectives for their relationship as well as a set of major projects that will bring significant—measurable—payoffs. But this is only the first step: the two firms must change many things in the ways they work internally as well as jointly.

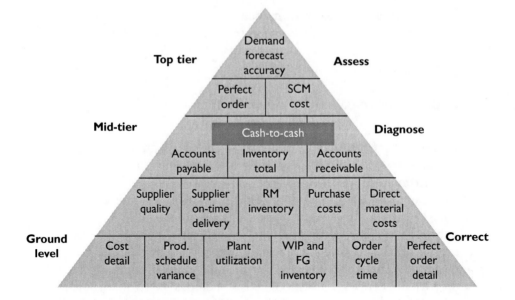

Figure 6.3 The hierarchy of supply chain metrics

Source: AMR Benchmark Analytix.

The two-sided staircase model

In Figure 6.4, we see a large consumer goods company working with a major supplier of packaging; the pair have used what we call the "two-sided staircase model" to frame their improvement agenda.

At the bottom of the staircase, we see the consumer goods firm (on the right) with the objective of a purchase price reduction, based on consolidating its procurement (reducing the supply base). On the supplier side (left), we see the packaging supplier as interested in this proposition, since through this agreement it expects to obtain economies of scale that would allow a volume-based price reduction. This, then, is the "what." The "how" is shown in the bubble in the middle of the figure. The two firms expect to execute this agreement through a standard relationship between purchasing and sales. In fact, this expectation is naïve.

✔ Some degree of product and process standardization will be

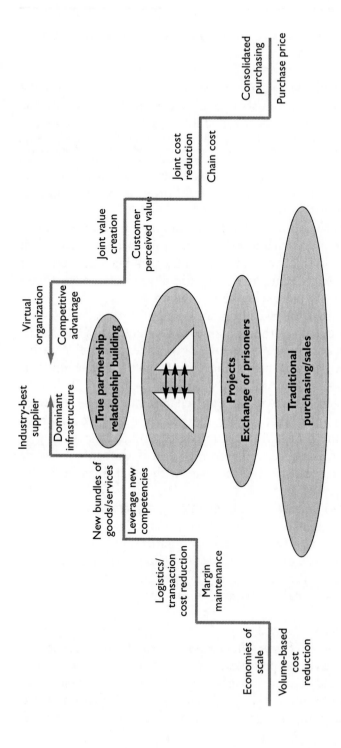

Figure 6.4 The two-sided staircase model for joint improvement

required across the two firms to make this more than new rottweiler games.

The second step in the improved relationship is depicted (on the right) as the consumer products firm now wishing to work with the supplier to achieve a joint cost reduction, which will take cost out of the chain (and reduce prices as a result). For the supplier, this might be interesting *if* together the companies can reduce logistics and transaction costs, *and* if the supplier can maintain its margins. But here, the "how" bubble is labeled "projects & exchange of prisoners."

The objectives for both customer and supplier are indeed achievable, but it will require hard work and new joint processes to in fact reduce logistics and transaction costs. It may well mandate someone from the supplier working full time for a year at the customer sites—and vice versa (an exchange of prisoners).

The third step that the two firms were able to foresee is to switch from the denominator to the numerator in value/cost. That is, the consumer goods company sees the next objective as jointly creating value, with its customers perceiving the product/service bundle as having higher value. What does the supplier think of this? Well, OK, it might say, but now we will have to redefine the bundle of goods and services we jointly create, with an expectation that we may both move up the value chain. We as suppliers are more than willing to do this if we can preserve our margins—and if we can gain some new competencies that we can leverage with other customers (we will get smarter).

But now, the joint work requirements are depicted as two triangles (the organizations on each side) with many linkages. The joint work will involve the two marketing organizations, engineering, manufacturing, and so on. The end result could be new transit packaging that is easier for the retailer to open and dispose of, or a package that the final consumer finds more environmentally desirable.

The last step foreseen by the two firms is vague at this early point in their collaborative efforts. The consumer goods firm sees it as a desire for a definitive competitive advantage that will be achieved by creating a "virtual organization"—some form of joint strategic objective. For the supplier, this game sounds good, if margins are at least maintained, competencies are leveraged, and the final result is becoming the industry's dominant packaging supplier (we are the smartest).

Pulling this off is shown as requiring a true partnership between the two firms, with significant efforts devoted to relationship-building at many levels in the two companies—with all that this implies: A major commitment and bigger undertaking. Both firms will need to keep the faith.

We have a fond memory of showing the two-sided staircase model to a senior purchasing executive in a large European electronics company. He came back to us and admitted that in his company there was only one side to the thinking: What the supplier needed to do next. We worked with this firm for several years to partially change their thinking. But in fairness, we must admit that we never truly succeeded. Purchasing in this company was always—and still is—driven by a rottweiler mentality and a single-minded focus on unit price reduction.

The tango is a complex dance

Many firms wish to achieve results similar to those depicted in Figure 6.4. We have seen several who have implemented major systems—such as enterprise resource planning (ERP) systems—and thereafter started endeavors "somewhat" similar to that depicted in the figure. But there has often been a big difference: Collaboration has had to start from a position that is strongly constrained by these systems, which have been installed with an internal company focus.

Figure 6.5 (overleaf) shows the problem. This is essentially the approach that Procter & Gamble tried to implement with several of its major suppliers a few years ago.

The customer (P&G in this case) creates plans in manufacturing, which yield a forecasted outflow of raw materials. This is passed to the supplier's sales organization, which proposes a replenishment shipment to the customer to be evaluated and confirmed. Thereafter, the supplier sales organization creates a consignment stock order that is picked and shipped to the customer. The supplier plans manufacturing to satisfy the proposed replenishment orders, based on the projected finished goods inventory balances. The shipments are received into raw materials inventory at the customer, and thereafter issued to manufacturing as needed. The issue is passed to the purchasing department to thereafter create a purchase order to

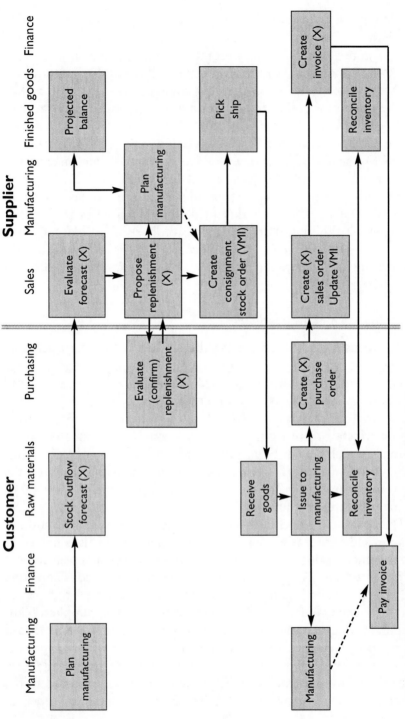

Figure 6.5 Extending lean with dyads: the BPR/IT challenge

match the quantity issued to manufacturing. This process essentially passes ownership of the goods from the supplier to the customer. On the supplier side, the receipt of the purchase order allows it to create a sales order and update the vendor-managed inventory account held by the customer. The sales order in turn passes to the finance function to create an invoice, which the customer pays. Also shown in Figure 6.5 is periodic joint inventory reconciliation between the customer and supplier.

Figure 6.5 includes (X) marks in many of the activity boxes. These are the transactions that could be eliminated with joint business process re-engineering work. The result is the customer's manufacturing plan passing directly to supplier manufacturing planning. The dotted arrow depicts the new linkage to create the stock order. Thereafter, the stock is picked and shipped to the supplier, and issued to manufacturing. Completion of manufacturing is now linked with another dotted line to finance, to pay the amount for the materials consumed. The differences are great. There are no longer sales orders, purchase orders, or invoices. All of these require human intervention in order to create them. Similarly, several human-intervention processes for shipments are eliminated.

It is obvious that the elimination of excess transactions is cost-effective. But the ERP systems in most companies are based on developing efficiency within a given business unit—without considering integration with customers and suppliers. They also satisfy standard accounting rules for matching transactions. As a result, they are not set up to operate without classic transactions such as sales orders, purchase orders, invoices, and classic payment procedures.

✔ Getting this couple to tango ain't gonna be easy!

A winning journey

We have developed a process for developing major improvements in carefully selected customer–supplier pairs. It encompasses a series of steps, in each case guided by their shared objectives. We, as disinterested third parties, go to people in both the customer and supplier organizations. We conduct structured but open-ended interviews, during which we ask them to tell "stories" about this customer/supplier: Which are the good, the bad, and the ugly? What do you like or dislike about working with the firm? Is it trust-worthy? What have been your good and bad experiences? What does the other firm do that costs you money?

The interviews typically take one to two hours, and it is rare to find someone who is less than forthcoming. Often at the end of the interview, the person will recommend that we speak with someone else—sometimes in his or her company, sometimes in the other one.

The questionnaire

After sifting the information gleaned from the interviews, we formu-late a preliminary set of conclusions, leading to a structured questionnaire, administered online. It is sent to as many people as possible, in both organizations, who might have opinions about working together. In each instance, the respondent is asked to rate the importance of the issue and then the extent to which it is being addressed and implemented.

Analysis of the results, both within a company and for the pair of firms, leads to important conclusions:

- Do the results support earlier conclusions?
- Is there general agreement on key issues?
- Where are the biggest differences?

The survey also introduces the improvement initiative to all people involved. It raises awareness and involves the people on the periphery of the customer–supplier pair.

Network mapping

A separate section of the questionnaire asks respondents to identify people they contact for inter-company issues. This supports creation of maps, depicting patterns of communication and those persons most influential in this collaboration.

Based on analysis of the questionnaire and network mapping, we develop tentative conclusions and a set of potential recommen-dations. These are a key input to the design of a subsequent work-shop. A written report is also prepared, since sometimes there are "hot buttons" that need to be considered. In one case, there was a delivery problem that had escalated to the senior management level in both companies. The senior executives did not want the collaborative initiative to become embroiled in what should be a short-term problem—one that had already had plenty of attention.

A key finding in almost every study is that the customer is more at fault than the supplier—the customer is not always right. Moreover, suppliers are reluctant to tell customers when they are wrong—or to be the messengers of bad news. The good news is that when customers are willing to admit that they are responsible for at least 50 percent of the problems, there is a great increase in supplier goodwill and enthusiasm for joint work.

The workshop

The workshop is run over two days, typically involving eight to ten people from each company. They arrive, having seen the preliminary conclusions, with relatively high hopes for a good outcome. Our role is to act as facilitators, independent third parties keeping the focus on the right issues and maintaining a steady pace through the two days. The workshop is structured to create maximum interaction, producing a clear set of agreed-upon actions, the logic behind those agreements, a plan for implementation of significant improvements in 6 to 12 months, and a set of personal commitments to make all this happen.

Seating is carefully planned to mix people from the two companies and place key decision makers next to each other. The workshop puts everything out in the open and develops complete transparency. The venue for the workshop is best at a neutral location—not too near either of the firms, so that everyone comes and stays for the duration. This gives the workshop an open and personable atmosphere.

A round-robin exercise is based on a set of individual interviews of four carefully chosen questions by four sub-groups of participants. The questions are designed to address the most important issues uncovered in the earlier phases. In one case, where there had been some serious arguments between one part of the customer organization and a particular supplier, one question was, "What are the problems we have encountered in the last year, and what do we need to do to keep them from recurring?"

The process for the round robin is that everyone answers every question, and each sub-group comes up with the consensus of the

entire group on each particular question. The overall result is a rank-
ing of the toughest issues facing the two firms. In practice, key executives are rarely surprised by the outcomes, but some important
nuances inevitably surface. Further, the result is not one pushed down
from the top—or pushed by customer onto supplier. The interviews'
personal nature fosters deeper knowledge and understanding of the
particular individuals in the pair of companies.

The workshop transformation exercise

At this point, there is a need to shift gears, from the problems to the
answers. The group is divided in two, and participants write on
sticky notes anything they can think of that should be done to
address the problems and issues examined so far. This process is
continued until the sub-group has run out of suggestions. The notes
are grouped and subsequently titled (which often has to be done two
or three times). Then, the answers from the two sub-groups are
combined, typically resulting in 10 to 15 groups of notes.

Thereafter, voting collects personal opinions about the most
important groups of proposed answers/initiatives. This typically
results in three to four clear winners—improvement ideas for which
there is a definitive consensus. Participants are asked to select the
idea on which they would like to work. The overall result is agreement on joint problems/issues, the potential solutions, shared vision
of what is most important, and a set of personal commitments to
make the necessary improvements.

We next base the facilitation on the "Deep Dive" process developed by the California design company Ideo, modified to focus on
the development of projects rather than products. The Deep Dive is
based on fast prototyping and a cycle of improvement efforts. It
always has the goal of defining something that is truly different—a
breakout project—that can be implemented in 6 to 12 months.

There is no formal expectation for the evening, except that the
participants stay together. Again, workshops away from home are
best. The participants discuss the improvement ideas and take the
time to get to know each other better; the value of this socializing
should not be underestimated. The second day begins with a very
short exercise, to amuse and set the stage for more cooperative
efforts. The teams now need to go again into the Deep Dive—
preparing a second (and perhaps third) prototype. In each case, the

result is again presented to the group at large for their suggestions. One of the workshop's final results is a detailed action plan:

- What are the deliverables?
- Who is to do what—and when? Milestones?
- How do we work together across the two companies?
- What are the resource requirements?
- Who needs to sign off and be involved?
- Is there some way to periodically renew our enthusiasm?
- And finally (un-stated), what is the role of key senior managers in going forward?

Results

The methodology has recently been applied in several firms, with well-received results. One firm made a major shift in manufacturing (and sourcing) from Western to Eastern Europe. In one instance, it was possible to identify (and thereafter align) a major difference in perceptions (on the part of the customer) about the capabilities of a large supplier. This was leading to a major confrontation that could easily have resulted in replacing what was a highly skilled and dedicated supplier with another of unknown abilities. This customer also had a significant problem with one of its largest makers of packaging materials. Here, we—as impartial third parties—were able to make a set of suggestions that have since allowed these two firms to enter into a significant development of new packaging products.

A somewhat different assignment involved a manufacturer in the food and beverage industry that was quite poorly evaluated by its two largest retail customers. By using the methodology here (somewhat tailored to the situation but essentially the same), it was possible to get the working relationship back on track. This firm was able to move from a rank of 15 out of 16 suppliers to a rank of 2—in less than six months.

We most recently applied the methodology to Bombardier Transport, where the senior management selected ten key suppliers. The first five were purposely chosen to be quite different, in order to test the concepts' robustness. Each of the pairs was able to successfully follow the process and implement major improvement efforts:

- In one case, standardization was enhanced with catalog pricing for determining the base price; thereafter, the size of the contract and combined contracts became the basis for final price negotiations. The volume for this supplier was significantly increased.

- In another quite different case, the supplier was in Poland. It was necessary to establish effective ways of working so that this supplier could have the right contacts with the various BT sites, while increasing its volume and determining the best product-line offerings for this company.
- Each of the other cases was similarly unique (a basic axiom of the method: Every customer–supplier relationship is unique). In each case, new levels of trust were established, win–win was seen as real, supplier volumes were increased, and new joint action programs were thereafter formulated.

So what?

Collaboration is not for the faint of heart, nor does it imply an end to hard work in finding better solutions. In some cases, those better solutions will come from new suppliers and/or customers. There will always be new firms with a better mousetrap, and your company must find and work with them. But the opportunities for improvements are fundamentally better in working with existing partner companies. The investments in trust, common language, working relationships, and mechanisms for problem resolution are already developed and should be possible to leverage. When new challenges occur, it is the best of these "marriages" that will come through with win–win solutions.

Delivering the bacon requires a great deal of work. Implied are some quite new ways to buy and sell, and even newer ways to link the buying and selling: to achieve the power of two. Your company should expect to make mistakes while traveling this avenue, but you need to learn from them—and keep going. Developing and nurturing pairs of aces mandates serious unlearning, and those leading the efforts must expect significant resistance.

Leadership will be necessary, as well as "umbrella holding" over those team members on the individual projects. It is important to keep track of the gains and publicize them widely. Cross-learning and comparisons are equally important, especially comparisons of buying efforts with selling efforts. Finally, those who deliver the bacon should be rewarded for their efforts.

Chapter 6 has been devoted to the "how:" How might your company undertake the journey leading to power of two payoffs? The next chapter takes on the task of institutionalizing customer—supplier partnerships, making collaboration a way of life in your company.

CHAPTER 7

Building the future

A partnership without an aggressive improvement agenda is no partnership at all. In essence, improved collaboration needs to become part of your firm's DNA. What this means in reality is the need to continually enhance the collaboration in key customer–supplier pairs: to make a pair of sevens into a pair of jacks, to make a pair of kings into a pair of aces, and to make this continual enhancement become a widely perceived strategic objective. In this chapter, our focus is on three important questions:

- What next?
- How do we maximize the rate of improvement?
- How do we institutionalize the process?

Bombardier Transport started its journey with five supplier firms. Five more were added the second year, and BT anticipates more in the future. This time the mix will shift to some suppliers and some customers. Each of these customer–supplier partnerships needs to continually move forward, periodically adopting a new improvement program. One pair has been working with a key supplier to develop standardization; this has been largely achieved, and the two firms now need to move on to new challenges. The next one will be to jointly reduce non-recurring costs.

Numico and Babynov have created a successful set of new baby food products; these incorporate clever design and new packaging with a marketing program targeted to children who would normally stop eating prepared baby food. The new products have been launched in the market-place, but the two firms now jointly face issues of ramp-up, delivery, capacity utilization, and well-timed information exchange.

The Rubik's cube of customer–supplier partnerships

Figure 7.1 depicts four critical issues for making a customer–supplier partnership a reality. Each of them is even more important in enhancing a partnership – that is, in making a pair of sevens into a pair of jacks.

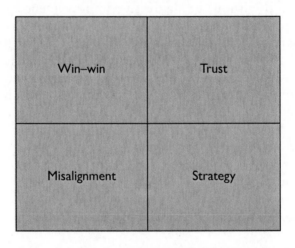

Figure 7.1 The Rubik's cube of customer–supplier partnerships

Each of these four issues implies an imperative. They need not only to exist but to be continually enhanced:

✔ Win–win takes on a new meaning and necessary new definition as the joint effort between customer and supplier evolves.

✔ So does trust—necessarily growing in depth, which supports new initiatives.

✔ Then there is strategic evolution: The strategic objectives must be expected to shift—for each of the partners as well as for the partnership.

✔ Finally, continually attacking and reducing misalignment is an ongoing part of the partnership process.

Making win–win real

In creating and maintaining a true win–win relationship, there is a natural tendency to overly consider your own problems and your own gains—and classic measurements reinforce this bias. Chapter 3 related a good example: a telecom firm wished to reduce its pipeline inventory with a major customer from more than 200 days to something like 75 days, and was surprised when the customer showed no enthusiasm for this great idea. There was nothing in it for the customer—in fact, more inventory allowed it to make last-minute adjustments to its building plans.

The natural win for a customer is joint cost reduction in the chain, which allows the price to be reduced—but this must not be achieved at the expense of supplier margins. The natural win for the supplier, in addition to margin preservation, is increased volume. However, these tend to be the first set of win–wins. The key issue is to update the win–wins for each new joint project, and to be clear on both sides that expectations are indeed being met.

For the Bombardier example cited above, the payoffs for standardization with a major supplier were definitively reduced prices, while the supplier's margins actually increased because of its ability to manufacture at significantly lower costs. But now, in switching to the objective of non-recurring cost reduction, the two firms need to make explicit many costs on both sides that have been hidden in prices, such as the time to prepare lengthy documents, respond to quotations, and argue over claims made by end customers. These often fall more on one side than the other and are difficult to assess, but not assessing them assumes they are unimportant—perhaps the worst possible assumption.

✔ Win–win needs to always be explicit—and continually updated.

For Numico, the win was innovation and new volumes, along with improving the company's image with retailers as providing new market opportunities. For its supplier, Babynov, the initial win was a new major customer with the associated volume increase, validation of a new product concept, and the experience of a product rollout in a new geographical area. But thereafter, the two firms needed to achieve savings in data collection/analysis, pipeline inventory reduction, improved scheduling and capacity utilization, and greater total sales for both firms. Again, achieving these goals required joint efforts and some means to keep track of who made the efforts and where the payoffs were manifested.

Second order win–win

We have described several good examples of successful customer–supplier partnerships, as well as some failures. We have also made a strong argument in favor of selected collaboration, in place of zero-sum-based supplier–customer relationships. But the key question is how to sustain and grow these relationships, if collaboration is to truly be part of a firm's DNA. What is needed to nurture a relationship? What will erode it, or kill it off?

The relationship between Hewlett-Packard and Canon has been touted as a great win–win example, with the unwritten rule at HP: screw it up and you are fired. But when HP bought Compaq, there was a new executive team. The CEO did not believe in the mythical relationship with Canon, and decided to start treating it like other suppliers. From the Canon side this was very upsetting: The two firms started to move into the zero-sum model, and the "marriage" was on the rocks. Fortunately for the relationship, this CEO left HP, and the partnership recovered. It is once again healthy.

So what is the key lesson here? Win–win needs to be seen in an overarching framework, one that is not subject to whim. DNA needs to be permanent. But in all of our examples (Bombardier, ABB–Caterpillar, Honda, HP, etc.) there is a constant risk that the win–win relationship will go off the tracks. In general, the longer the partnership has existed, the better are its chances of continuing. Those most new are at greatest risk, since the DNA is not as deep or as shared among all the people in both firms. The appeal of former ways of thinking and operating are closer to hand.

But there is more than time of the partnership. Complacency can go hand in hand with time. There must be a continual search for new levels of win–win, and each firm must compare these with its other alternatives. The HP–Canon special relationship can only stay special if both HP and Canon continue to see clear benefits accruing, and these exceed those that might be gained by working with others. The same holds true for BT, ABB and all the other examples: "Marriage" needs to be better than "divorce," but there are many reasons why it should be. There is a collective joint investment in working relations that can and must be capable of continuous improvement, as well as leverage to achieve new heights. Achieving new heights requires ongoing investment in time and energy: An aggressive improvement agenda needs to be established—and achieved!

Creating/nurturing trust

Trust is perhaps the most important of all four imperatives, the hardest to maintain, and the least obvious to define and assess. There is also typically a large difference between what is expressed as an overall feeling, and the reality. In one recent example, senior executives in both firms felt they had achieved a reasonable partnership and good results. A new working arrangement had led to a significant increase in volume with major business for this supplier—business that was originally expected to go to a competitor. However, many in the customer company were suspicious that this increased volume would lead to monopolistic behavior by the supplier. And on the supplier side, there were feelings that the extra business must have been achieved at lower margins, meaning that the customer would surely apply further cost squeezes. The key message here is that trust will always need to be enhanced—continuous improvement requires it.

Trust, like win–win, has increasing levels of depth and requirements. Even more important, trust has a similar need for joint investment and a sense of fairness. If the customer asks for some measure of trust from the supplier, it must expect to reciprocate—perhaps without being asked. A bad example we often see is customers asking for all sorts of additional information from a supplier, including detailed cost breakdowns, while at the same time not accurately sharing known demand information—and making minimal commitments for future business. This behavior reduces trust rather than increasing it.

When a customer–supplier partnership means making a pair of sevens into a pair of jacks, the level of joint trust needs to be greatly expanded. This can easily become the major hindrance to achieving stronger partnerships. The trust required to jointly implement a standardization program is significant, but going beyond to tackle non-recurring costs is much more fundamental. Most companies will surely resist replacing complex legal documents with less formal approaches, but you truly need to ask why. Some years ago, one of us worked with Ethan Allen. Co-founder and then CEO, Nat Ancell, based all contracts with franchised dealers on a handshake; he said:

✔ If the guy is an SOB, no amount of paper will help.

Second-order trust

What are the fundaments of trust? How does one move beyond platitudes? How is trust nurtured, and how is it most easily broken? Our most important observation here is how deeply trust resides in the eye of the beholder. Most people are innately suspicious, and any unexpected action by the other party in the relationship tends to be seen negatively. Similarly, most people tend to believe they are operating with the best of intentions, and everyone else can easily see that this is the case.

These observations are a potential train wreck to any partnership, so they need to be mitigated. Trust tends to be developed both top-down and bottom-up. It is critical for senior level executives to meet socially and develop an ease/understanding with counterparts. In general we have seen this occur when there is a particular issue at hand, such as the ABB–Caterpillar turbocharger interaction. There was a group who established "governance" and this established the initial top-down linkage. The bottom-up occurred when there were concrete issues assigned to cross-company teams to resolve.

But the top-down and bottom-up trust had to be augmented when the focus shifted to more than immediate turbocharger issues. The process by which this takes place needs to become as clearly defined as possible. It should not be left to chance and be the sole result of specific cross-company issues. The top-down should bubble up to more senior people on both sides, and the bottom-up needs to spread as needed. Both need to be driven with a shared vision and purpose: The two firms believe in this partnership, they can continually demonstrate new win–win results, and specific executives are openly committed to furthering the collaborative relationship because it is the best interests of their company.

Building partnership strategy

The importance of shared vision and common strategy for the partnership is the third of our four imperatives. If a customer and supplier do not see the road ahead in a consistent way—one in which they are both better off through working collaboratively—then the partnership will probably never go beyond a pair of threes. The two firms must truly believe that by working together they can create a much stronger core competence than they could by working independently. Building the future through enhanced partnerships requires an ongoing process of identifying new strategic objectives—and the detailed projects required to achieve them.

In Chapter 1, we described the "super-supplier" relationship that has been developed by Honda and a few of its key suppliers. These are clearly pairs of aces that incorporate carefully integrated strategic decisions and operations. The payoffs largely come from integrated operations that use the suppliers' capacities at very high utilization rates, supported by rapid (and full) information exchange. Enhancements focus on ways in which the most expensive assets in the chain can be "sweated" at even higher levels, as well as when to add more assets and how to sweat these as well.

Strategic integration requires both an overall shared vision/sense of direction, and a clearly articulated set of objectives for each major improvement project. In each case, the win–win needs to be well understood and *achieved,* the trust needs to be enhanced as necessary, and the two firms need to communicate the new initiative as being a strategic objective for mutual advantage. In both companies, this viewpoint will need to be explained—much more than once. Nokia's mandate for "shared values" epitomizes this imperative. If Nokia and a supplier do not see the world ahead in a common way, there is no point in trying to form a partnership. Whether or not it seems to work in the short run, without shared objectives, the necessary continual enhancements cannot be realized. Nokia's efforts are better expended with another supplier or customer.

Second-order partnership strategy

Key issues in partnership strategy need to focus on framing the agenda for the future: What is the win–win, both immediate and long-term? What can the two firms achieve jointly that is significantly better than either can achieve alone? How do you put this into a set of projects and assign the key people to make each of them a reality?

- What new product opportunities should Hewlett-Packard and Canon identify? Which are short-term and which are long-term? What are the specific benefits that each firm will achieve if the developments are a success?
- What should Bombardier and Knorr-Bremse do next? What are the ways in which they might jointly transform the after-sales service market for train maintenance? Capture the Chinese market? What are some short-term objectives, such as a joint bid on a new large train project?
- What should Honda and its steel parts supplier do next? Should the supplier now outsource some of the easier parts to concentrate on more complex stampings? Should the two firms jointly design some new metal parts? What processes at Honda are better developed at the supplier?
- What competencies does Nokia—and its supply chain—need to develop for the future? With which "magic ten" partners should it form a very intense partnership?

Managing misalignment

We use the term *misalignment* here rather than *alignment*, because this is what must be expected. There will always be misalignment, and it needs to be effectively managed. Doing so is a key part of the "grease" needed to run the continuous improvement engine. Every person in the customer company will have his or her own opinion about the supplier, based on history, war stories, folklore, or rumor. The same holds for the supplier side: People will remember various stories—even when untrue—and repeat and even embellish them over time. The key is to keep these opinions in bounds and to quickly act when they become disruptive. It is important to influence this pattern positively—to create "good stories."

Another term for what is needed here is *untangling*. Every customer–supplier relationship has a history as well as perceptions as to what happened, who was at fault for various things, and who can or cannot be trusted. There is a natural tendency to blame others, particularly those at a greater distance. It is healthy to get as much of this as possible out in the open, sort it out, and strive for a blame-free environment. We have found that having an ombudsman for both the customer and supplier companies can be very useful. The role of the ombudsman is to continually look for misalignment and settle issues quickly and positively.

Another concept that seems to work well is the establishment of a council made up of key suppliers. They in turn share best practices and make improvement suggestions to the customer. These might be in terms of new processes, or they can provide insights into misalignment issues and how they might be resolved.

✔ Untangling is most easily accomplished when the tangles are small.

Second-order misalignment management

Second-order misalignment issues need to focus on the ways in which conflicts can be avoided in the first place, and ways to overcome the natural resistance to greatly increasing the level of joint activity between customer–supplier partners.

- As ABB fulfills its goal of increasing its sales to Caterpillar from $50 million to $500 million, it will be necessary for a vast number of people in both firms to not only understand this move, but support it—because it is very much in the interests of both firms to do so. This implies, first and foremost, that stage 1 in Chapter 2 is never violated: Flawless execution of whatever the partners decide to do is absolutely essential. Moreover, each such effort needs to be seen as a win–win, because this can be clearly demonstrated: This partnership is superior to any other way to support Caterpillar objectives. As the business between the two firms expands, more and more people will need to become convinced and committed, sequentially. This implies the need for a carefully sculpted proactive approach to managing misalignment.
- A similar set of issues faces Nestlé as it implements its Project Globe. Internally, everyone needs to first accept, then believe in

the importance of operating as an integrated unit. But it is even more critical to thereafter adopt an integrated supply chain. This implies changing hearts and minds: At Nestlé, at key suppliers, and at key customers.

Driving the procurement agenda

At least half of the work in enhancing customer–supplier partnerships involves major changes in procurement. In fact, our experience leads to the conclusion that it is significantly more than half. Many firms have had to clean house in their procurement organization, or at least, have had to develop definitively different sets of strategic objectives for supplier partners, find ways to separate the rottweilers from the collaborative work, determine who does what, and create different metrics for the two groups. In order to "build the future," it is imperative to go beyond a few pilot programs in partnership—and unlearn many aspects of classic procurement.

Establishing the culture

Moving from a procurement culture based on combative approaches to one with a mixture of combative and collaborative creates a certain amount of organizational schizophrenia. Classic negotiation strategy dictates that procurement people be tough with all suppliers, but now this approach needs to be split into combative and collaborative. Managing the two approaches simultaneously is not easy, and the senior procurement managers must establish differing modes of behavior, conduct, and performance measures.

The expectation is that the relative proportion of procurement (in terms of total purchasing spend) will shift toward collaborative relations, but this movement needs to proceed in a controlled fashion. Getting too enthusiastic about collaboration can lead to a situation in which some suppliers will take advantage of what they perceive as a weaker negotiating position. This can be overcome only by making partnerships one by one, where the win–win is clearly articulated and achieved in every case, and where the subsequent steps in continuous enhancement are also unambiguously defined. At each of these steps, the Rubik's cube of partnership depicted in Figure 7.1 needs to be enhanced: The additional win–win must be clear—as the additional trust requirements for the next stage must be—the strategic objectives must be well defined, and managing the inevitable misalignment is imperative.

It is also important to recognize the necessary shifts in tactics, work, and allocations of resources. The expectation is that over time, procurement will significantly reduce its supplier base (by 75 percent is a good rule of thumb). Furthermore, standardization efforts should reduce the number of items purchased by another 75 percent. All this takes time, effort, human resources, commitment, new ways of working, and a new set of relationships with both internal functions and functions in the supplier partner.

Very similar change conditions exist for sales and marketing: As a supplier, you need to understand your customers' objectives, their strategy, and how to help them achieve these. You must act in ways that foster trust and untangle misalignments before they cause major problems. And win–win means helping your customer part-ners to see how you have jointly achieved key goals—and are ready to establish new ones.

The leadership requirements for moving procurement into a mix of combative and collaborative relationships are critical. The senior procurement managers need to have a mandate from on high, and the determination and staying power to carry out the necessary changes. Sales and marketing face an equally challenging agenda: Segmenting the customers, choosing which are most possible to work with mutually, continually evaluating progress, and setting continuing new objectives.

In both procurement and sales, there is a natural tendency to advocate "partnership" in too many cases. If a firm is known to have favored customers, then each customer wishes to be so desig-nated. So does each salesperson for his/her clients. The same problem exists for suppliers. Everyone wishes to be designated as special and deserving of extra efforts. But this cannot be. We have made the argument for ten many times, and we stick to it.

It may be OK however to "call" many customers or suppliers "partners"—provided you are clear about what this really means.

Supporting key individuals

Eventually, certain people will be able to deliver on the partnership promise but many will not. One part of the leadership challenge is to find and motivate those who can make the shift in strategy as well as practice. To some extent, this requires "holding an umbrella" over their heads while they do the new work, insulating them from the predominant culture and ways of working.

Some people in your organization will fight this effort, either openly or in secret. These may be good candidates for early retirement, but if a few can be brought around to see the light, they can be quite influential in convincing the other resistors. In fact, the opposite problem can occur with some procurement managers who strongly endorse it. The early adopters are unlikely to fully appreciate the scale of the overall change process. What all of this means for the senior procurement managers is a need to carefully (and continually) sort the sheep from the goats, to expect mistakes, and to be ready to recover as necessary. There will be a continuing imperative to determine who is delivering the goods and who is not. Similar arguments apply to sales and the customer side.

It is critical that supplier–partnership development not be viewed as a job solely for procurement people. In Figure 6.4 of Chapter 6, we presented the two-sided staircase model for joint improvement. The cast of characters involved at each step of the staircase necessarily changes for both the consumer products company and the packaging supplier. Furthermore, procurement people play a relatively minor role in the overall series of transformation steps. It will always be individuals, working in cross-functional and cross-organizational project teams, that deliver the promise. They have to be motivated, led, measured, and rewarded. But delivering the promise can be rewarding.

Creating segments, segments, and segments

Building the future requires a continuing assessment of the supplier and customer bases:

- Which suppliers are delivering the goods?
- Which customers are most likely to dominate their markets?
- With which ones are we ready to move on to a new improvement project?
- Should our present classification of suppliers and customers continue?
- Are any of these becoming complacent?

In fact, it is critical to not permit complacency to develop in a partnership—it is the beginning of the end.

Each supplier–customer relationship must be continually questioned. This is a two-sided investigation: Either party can cause complacency—and it is both of their faults, regardless of the cause. A good customer–supplier partnership is an investment, one that should—must—deliver a clearly articulated objective. The time that individuals have invested in making a partnership work must not be squandered. This time, expended by your company's smartest and most motivated people, is your most important resource—usually much scarcer than money.

A related issue: Is each of your key suppliers still providing the bundles of goods and services you need as the customer? Sometimes the technology shifts, and an existing supplier is simply no longer able to provide what is required. Essentially the same problem arises when a new potential supplier arrives bearing a price offer significantly lower than that of the existing supplier (Bombardier calls this a "wild card"). There is an obvious issue of loyalty here but, additionally, one of implied complacency: Why did the partners (*both* of them) not anticipate the change in technology and see whether the existing supplier could develop it—and thereby continue to leverage the win–win relationship (whose "assets" are much more than technology)? Why was the partnership surprised by the much lower-cost offer? Were they not benchmarking properly?

✔ Surprises are welcome only on your birthday.

If we go back to the super-supplier relationship we described in Chapter 1 between Honda of America and its sheet metal supplier, it is virtually impossible for a rational bid to underprice that of the super supplier. The supplier utilizes the absolute state-of-the-art technology and operating processes, and the partnership sweats those assets at a high rate of capacity utilization. How can anyone achieve lower costs?

The super-supplier ideas also support the win–win dimension of the Rubik's cube. Honda achieves a much lower cost structure than its competitors. However, it also wants its super supplier to sell to these competitors—at significantly higher market prices! Honda can—and should—help its supplier do so. This is "fair," since Honda and the supplier have jointly designed out many costs as well as improving the numerator in the value/cost ratio. The firm with a pair of aces supplier relationship wants its supplier partner to increase its margins—at the expense of the customer's competitors.

Making innovation the big game

Utilizing supplier brainpower to support innovation can, in many cases, provide the truly great source of competitive advantage. Joint R&D is, obviously, one means to this end. Many electronics firms have worked jointly with integrated circuit manufacturers to develop chips that allow advanced product features. A more powerful concept comes from the ideas around value chain positioning, as explained in Chapter 6. In essence, the customer and supplier need to continually search for the winning combination for the customer—with its customers (the enhanced bundle of goods and services)—and then jointly work to develop this combination. This will typically involve outsourcing: Who is best equipped to do what? How might we bring new products to market sooner? Who should buy raw materials? Who has the lowest cost of capital—and therefore should finance various investments?

A major issue in customer–supplier partner innovation concerns which partner should be concentrating on which areas of research. How will the specialization and integration develop over time—particularly as the supplier moves up the value chain and the customer outsources more of the value to the supplier, and the supplier becomes more of a systems integrator? Additionally, what are the new research directions for the customer?

These questions again reinforce the importance of the Rubik's cube. Without win–win, trust, shared strategy, and management of misalignment, none of this is possible. In joint innovation, there will be key issues of intellectual property, confidentiality, and exclusivity. All of these can be addressed—and leveraged for joint benefit—only by having the basics in place.

The purchasing agenda can also include finding innovative ways to increase the product line. Thus, at Hewlett-Packard, purchasing asks sales what they wish they had to sell that HP lacks time to design and make. Purchasing then finds suppliers interested in designing these items, to be sold under the HP brand.

Another clever idea in which purchasing increased the firm's competencies in innovation was implemented by Numico, which went to each of its major suppliers with the following question: "Suppose we buy $1 million per year, and in your annual report you state that you spend 10 percent of sales on R&D. This means that we are paying $100,000 per year for your research. How might we create a win–win based on joint R&D to win the end customers?

Pushing sales and marketing

Power-of-two payoffs need to be driven from two directions—jointly. Purchasing is not the only area that needs to make major changes. We have noted in several places that purchasing needs to embrace reverse marketing and sales, and marketing and sales needs to embrace reverse purchasing.

> ✔ What are your objectives and practices in making partnerships with customers? With suppliers? Why is there any difference?

Facing the challenges in key account management

Key account management is a popular approach to sales and marketing in many firms. We have examined how it is working for ABB and other firms. But now, in light of the Rubik's cube ideas, key account management needs to also play a policy role in creating the future. What is needed is an activity that develops and enlarges an overall view of each key customer, rather than separating the activity among business units that have little or no understanding of the overall situation. This is easier said than done. In the end, the business units have bottom-line responsibility, do not wish to give up contact with what they regard as important customers, are not particularly interested in their impact on other business units, and certainly do not wish to have a key account manager (KAM) making decisions that adversely impact their business units in order to optimize the overall business activity.

But some sort of key account focus needs to reside within the Rubik's cube approach:

- What is the next level of win–win—for the company and this customer? What are the products, the joint-technology roadmaps, the approaches needed? Which business units need to be involved?

- What are the new trust elements needed? Who needs to get on board? Who in the present way of working can best inform these people about the processes used and the thinking that must be developed?
- What is the shift in joint strategy you and the customer need to adopt? Is this a fundamentally new set of business interests with new people, or an improvement on present workings? Is this a shift from one collaborative stage to another? If so, do you have the resources to pull it off?
- How can you best refine your approach to misalignment? Where might you most likely run into problems? Do you have the right ombudsman resources? Who are the key executives on both sides who will own this new endeavor?

Finally, there is the ongoing need to sort out thorny issues such as where a KAM should be based and to whom he or she should report. Although any form of organization can be made to work with the right leadership and attitude, we often find that this role is assigned to the existing salesperson in the business unit with the highest volume. This has major potential problems. Primarily, this person needs to "unlearn" past behavior that optimizes payoffs to the existing business unit. The KAM needs to represent the entire company now, not just one unit. It is optimization for the company—not the business units individually. It is critical that fairness in this regard be widely perceived in both the supplier and customer organizations.

Making this a reality is not easy. When a KAM resides in one business unit, there is pressure to sell its products, push initiatives that this unit favors, resist ones that will cause it problems, not "waste" funds traveling to customer sites that do no business with this unit, and generally keep the unit at the center of the customer relationship. To the extent that other units perceive any of these conditions, the effectiveness of the KAM concept is diminished.

Key account management is most effective when the KAM becomes the voice of the customer in his or her organization. This implies knowing what the existing challenges are in the key account—and how best to help the customer surmount these challenges. Doing so requires an ability to call on all the business units' resources, coordinating them, and integrating them with the right people at the customer. Best practice will enable the KAM to know more about the customer than anyone else in his or her organization. But the KAM also needs to know the abilities and competencies of the individual business units. This includes a network of knowledgeable people as well as key decision makers:

✔ Who needs to say yes?

The other side of the coin

It goes without saying that key account management requires a matching attitude on the part of the customer. There is simply no point in proposing a true key account management relationship to a customer with only rottweiler approaches to dealing with suppliers. But this is only a very basic qualifier. Pushing key account management as the basis for evolving into stage 4 collaborative relationships requires equally significant changes on the customer side—going way beyond issues in purchasing.

If the KAM at the supplier is to be the point person for finding/exploiting the white space at the customer, there is a concomitant role for such a person at the customer side: what are the technologies, knowledge, and other competencies at this supplier—and how might you make good use of them? What has to change in your company to make this a reality?

There will be a natural negative attitude on the part of the customer toward this idea: What is in this for them—or their business unit? Why should they give their business to the supplier of another business unit that they do not know well? In fact, what this shows is the clear imperative for a well articulated win–win. The customer business unit should do this *because* it is a clear win for your company. The supplier company needs to help prove this.

Who are the customer senior managers that need to take ownership? Where are the major roadblocks, and how can they be removed—and who needs to do this?

Again, turning to building the future and the role of the Rubik's cube, there are equal challenges (opportunities) on the customer side:

- What does long-term win–win look like from your side? What are your objectives in terms of supply base reduction, direct and indirect cost savings, supplier support for new product introduction, joint top-line development, and new markets?

- What are the key elements in trust that will be needed to support the future degree of collaboration? What is a realistic assessment of the present trust levels? What will be needed to reach your objectives? What are the major roadblocks on your side as well as that of the supplier?
- What is the match in strategic directions for this supplier and your company? Is there a potential conflict that needs to be resolved sooner rather than later? Is there sufficient clarity on intellectual property, confidentially, exclusivity, and supply to your competitors?
- What are the mechanisms on your side to manage misalignment? Are they sufficient? What that is new is needed—on both sides? Can you anticipate where issues will come up and find ways to forestall them?
- When you are done, what are the lessons learnt, and how can these be widely distributed in your company—and in the supplier's?

We are entering a somewhat new area of management here, but it seems there needs to be a person or activity that mirrors key account management on the customer side. Such a person could come from procurement, although experience in marketing might be even better. In the end, the objective should be to determine how collaborative efforts with this key supplier can be best leveraged to win the hearts of your customer base.

Developing solutions buying and selling

Moves up the value chain should not only be initiated by the customer. Sales and marketing people need to sell these ideas to their customers. You want the customers to outsource more to you—to generate more sales and to increase your incumbency with the customer—while staying above the commodity level. This implies selling problem solutions, developing bundles of goods and services in which the whole is more than the sum of the parts.

✔ The bundle needs to continually evolve—to provide enhanced solutions.

A common procurement practice is to dissect the cost of an assembly or other solution, determining the "should cost" of each component. The sum of these is then considered the "should cost" of the solution. The supplier's solution will almost always look bad in this comparison.

We recently witnessed just such an example for one of Bombardier Transport's suppliers. This supplier manufactured several key components that could be purchased separately, as well as a large assembly that included these components as well as others. BT appreciated the supplier's technical competencies, but it deemed the price quotations for the assemblies to be too high. As a result, BT purchased all the components and made the assemblies itself. The supplier felt that BT's calculation approach was faulty: It did not include costs of design, testing, warranties, and various transactions. Our conclusion was that the supplier had failed to prove its value proposition to BT: It needed to show conclusively why the whole was indeed more than the sum of the parts. Furthermore, it was critical for this supplier to view the systems solution through BT's eyes—what can it do for its customer?—rather than as a product that the supplier believes is good for BT.

We see providing solutions as exactly what a good supplier should be doing, continually tailoring those solutions to better support its key customers' value propositions. This imperative has two parts. First, the supplier must truly be able to create a solution definitively superior to anything the customer can develop itself. The superiority might be cost-based or technical, although the latter is usually more interesting. A cost-based advantage might, however, come from the customer outsourcing a system that allows it to eliminate some significant support activities, such as logistics, testing, engineering, or procurement. The second imperative is to the sales and marketing organization:

✔ If all you can do is sell on price, you are not doing your job.

Making total cost of ownership real

We have noted in several places how difficult it is to sell an enhanced bundle of goods and services to a customer that is interested only in unit price. But this raises an extension to the last admonition to sales and marketing: If you truly have a lower total cost of ownership solution, you should be able to sell it. You need to figure out how, who needs to help, and how you can demonstrate the value proposition. Don't simply accept the false set of present constraints.

It is up to the supplier to be sure that the solution is indeed evaluated in terms of total cost of ownership. It is far too easy to just establish potential costs of components without taking into account the solutions design, costs of assembly, downstream warranty costs, inventory holding costs, etc.

This means that BT needs to sell rail operators the improved equipment that will yield lower maintenance costs. If this necessitates some new complex financial arrangements, so be it. If it requires a senior management to senior management relationship, make it happen.

✔ If there are those who will not listen, suggest they consider early retirement.

We believe that if you as a supplier can provide a bundle of goods and services that offers a truly lower total cost of ownership (TCO), and you cannot sell it, you need some new sales and marketing people!

But we must not stop here. There is another TCO issue that need not include the end customers. It is too easy to say that because the rail operators or some other end customers are interested only in the original equipment price, there is no room for TCO. There is a TCO issue between every supplier and customer pair. These costs can be readily identified and sharply reduced through joint actions. We have already noted many of them: transaction costs, inventories, complex contractual documents, double engineering efforts, under-utilized capacity, extra testing, negotiations, warranties, field failures, repair costs, poor quality, unnecessary quality, scheduling, and non-flawless execution. This is a veritable gold mine. Key parts of it should be explicitly included in the supplier's value proposition—and *sold* by its sales and marketing organization. Again, these people may face rottweiler mentalities at their customer, but these are not an excuse. If the TCO is truly there, it can surely be tapped.

Getting beyond customer relationship management

Far too many firms have invested huge sums in customer relationship management (CRM), thinking that having more data will allow them to do wondrous things. In fact, these systems often end up being designed by information technology people, who all too often know little about customers. The result is usually a mountain of data with limited relevance. CRM does indeed offer help for some routine problems, such as keeping track of who is visiting the customer, how much it is buying, and how well it is meeting contractual obligations for payment terms. But in other cases, where the focus is on more unique bundles, the value is limited.

✔ We recently asked one company's senior marketing person his need for CRM. His reply was that on a list of 100 top priorities, it would be number 103.

A recent article (Meyer and Schwager 2007) makes a nice distinction between customer relationship management and customer experience management. The former focuses on what the company knows about a customer, the latter on what a customer thinks about the company. The difference in approach is fundamental, supporting our earlier argument about being approximately right rather than exactly wrong, and understanding that it is perceptions that are often more important than facts.

An interesting manifestation of this phenomenon (facts versus perceptions) is the common practice of collecting data on delivery performance and interpreting these as measures of customer satisfaction. Recall the Ethiopian Airlines anecdote presented in Chapter 6: It had the industry's best on-time departure performance because it kept changing the departure times until the planes left the ground. When the customer wants products now, data on meeting your delivery promises seem irrelevant. It may well be that problems in delivery performance are caused by customer behavior (they wake up in a new world every morning). However, this has little to do with their perceptions of how well you as a supplier are meeting their needs.

Making it all work

Our major theme in this chapter has been continuous transformation of key customer–supplier partnerships. There can be—as we have said many times in this book—only a few pairs of aces, but these few will provide a great competitive edge. These pairs are with suppliers, and they are with customers. There should be no inherent difference in approach. There needs to be a clear win–win for both parties, and the game is never over. The pair must always look for the next challenge, and determine how it can jointly be surmounted. In this last section, we briefly identify several key issues that support development of customer–supplier partnerships.

Leadership

It goes without saying that partnerships are impossible unless senior management believes in them—that is, unless management sees customer–supplier collaboration as an imperative for developing competitive advantage. But there is much more here than the old "top management support" baloney. There need to be clear champions in the company, in all of the key functions. Senior marketing people need to see true customer partnerships as the best way to compete, be willing to assign top people to KAM roles, be ready to redefine relative positions on the value chain, and will when necessary take short-term hits to achieve long-term goals.

The most senior person in procurement must be a true believer. This means abandoning classic behaviors with a few key suppliers, and finding the ways to jointly support pair of aces development. He or she must be ready to hear proposals from suppliers for new value propositions and how the two companies might jointly gain from them. This executive needs to help the key suppliers use their capacities most intently, best matching customer needs with optimum supplier capacity utilization. It will also be necessary to help create and continuously improve the set of metrics by which the partnership can be evaluated, ensuring that win–win is never just a set of empty words. This person will need to hold the umbrella over the early pairs, protecting them from the rottweilers in the organization who will be critical. He/she needs to hold true to promises made to key suppliers, even when this means taking a hit. Finally, and most fundamentally, this person needs to lead the revolution in thinking/attitudes in procurement: *The key suppliers are not your enemies.*

Engineering is another function in which major changes are possible and in which the payoffs can be large. The chief engineer needs to be open-minded about working with engineers in customer and supplier firms. There will necessarily be assignments of key personnel to major projects, such as standardization, which will require large human resource expenditures. Through all of this, you need to maintain a long-term view, resisting daily pressures to utilize engineering talent to deal with immediate crises.

The same kinds of commitments are required in other functional areas, but in the end it is the most senior level where the rubber meets the road. They simply *must* buy in. If their commitment is anything less than total, it will be immediately so perceived throughout the organization, leading to failure.

We recently met with the CEO of a key supplier firm, who had a strong reputation as being a tough guy who was disinclined to suffer fools lightly. We ended up having a great discussion, and the word spread like wildfire through his company. When we met the CEO at the customer site, we told him this, and said, "It's now up to you. You can either make this or break it, but everyone will look to you to see what you will do." He too bought in.

This was, of course, only the beginning, not the end, but the joint work is now more than a year old, with results that no one would have predicted.

Governance again

Leadership needs to be manifested in processes that drive behavior as well as concrete results. Collaboration will not happen by itself. Best practice establishes some governance process to periodically evaluate progress, raise any issues, and re-energize the relationship. Senior representatives need to meet periodically. The meetings need to resolve issues and report on specific project progress, but more importantly, they must be about networking. The senior people on both sides need to decide when others should be brought into the meetings, perhaps because a future problem situation could use a head start—before the issues are even articulated. When meetings are called because of the other party's perceived bad behavior, it is an uphill effort, typically beginning with a bad climate, little trust, a great deal of misalignment, and serious zero-based thinking.

This was exactly the situation when ABB and Caterpillar started with their KAM approach. There was considerable animosity on the part of Caterpillar toward ABB, based on a perception of poor support, which the KAM failed to understand until a senior management meeting between the two firms. Significant remedial actions were immediately instituted, there was a meeting of minds between two key individuals, and they drove the change process. In less than three years, business between ABB and Caterpillar doubled.

The key executives meet periodically, and problems may or may not come up. If things are going well, the problems should be mitigated on a day-to-day basis. In fact, this group told us that they almost never look at their contracts—it is just not necessary.

Another example of governance is Lenovo, which has developed a "procurement ombudsman"—any supplier can contact this individual at any time with any problem relating to the company's purchasing practices. This is an overall approach, applicable to all the suppliers, but some enhanced version of it could be applied to a company's key suppliers. As recounted in Chapter 4, the CEO of Reckitt Benckiser gave each of the company's top 20 suppliers a new mobile phone with one number already stored—his.

Facilitation

The final ingredient essential to making customer partnerships a reality is a facilitation process. We have found in our work that we, as outside third parties, can break through many entrenched perceptions and bad feelings. In one case, we started with a customer and supplier in the midst of two significant lawsuits. The supplier was astonished to be given the suggestion of going through the process we described as "a winning journey" in Chapter 6. But they went through with it, and the two firms are now on a totally new course. Both are delighted and have pledged significant human resources to jointly find solutions to three or four key challenges.

So what?

Building the future requires a serious ongoing effort. Power of two partnerships require a great deal of work to obtain pair of aces results. The four dimensions of the Rubik's cube must be continually assessed, but on the basis of ever-greater challenges being put to the partnership. Both customer and supplier need to see the key partnerships as their best source of competitive advantage. They need an evaluation system, metrics, and process to periodically be sure they are working at maximum effort on the right issues.

Let us not underestimate the challenges these partnerships pose for changing attitudes and behaviors. Leadership is required at many levels, and individual project assignments will have major stretch objectives. But having seen some of the results, we can only say how exciting it is to experience.

In the end, both customers and suppliers need to recognize that *the power of two* is the best way to survive in today's competitive environment—working jointly and creatively to continually increase their joint strategic advantage.

This chapter has been devoted to some key issues in making collaboration a real part of your company. It is not easy, and there are built-in roadblocks, but the payoffs are real. In the next chapter, we turn explicitly to the issue of change management—but now with a focus on joint change—in both the customer and supplier firms.

CHAPTER 8

Changing two at a time

This chapter examines an expanded role for change management: Considering the joint changes needed to create pairs of aces. There is a vast literature on change management and the best practices for transforming organizations. Similarly, there has been a great deal of attention given to the organizational issues associated with key account management and global account management. However, this is largely for one firm, not two jointly. We will briefly review the key concepts in each of these areas, but our objective is to go significantly beyond this thinking.

The literature on change management and global account management is largely devoted to the organizational issues that play out in one company. Our focus is on those that must play out in two companies simultaneously. Deciding on the best approach to global account management must be based on the unique changes needed in both the customer and the supplier organization.

✔ Concentrating on one is like clapping with one hand.

This is not a one-size-fits-all program. The changes will be unique to each key customer pair, and will change over time. The change processes are ongoing.

From one-sided to two-sided change

Collaborative relationships do not happen by themselves. Significant changes are required, and it is extremely important to avoid myopia in thinking about those changes. Pair of aces development requires broad-based change by both the buyer and the seller. Although after reading seven chapters about the power of two you might think that an obvious statement, we have found many sourcing executives surprised the first time they hear it. A typical reaction is, "But this is supplier development. The supplier must change—but you mean *we* must change too?" An obvious example is in outsourcing situations, in which the customer needs to shift internal competencies to a supplier.

Let us run through the key issues by examining a change management model, and then see how the efforts must shift dramatically when applied to pairs.

A classic organizational change model

Figure 8.1 is a model often used by one of our IMD colleagues to exemplify the process of organizational change. The starting position is the establishment of the new *desired state*, the one the organization should achieve. This desired state is not only the goals or strategic objectives—it also explicitly recognizes the new behaviors needed in the organization, as well as changes needed in the design of the organization. For example, to implement Six Sigma would require new patterns of work, changes in the roles of leaders, new organization structure, deployment of new tools, and so on. All of this would require changes in the behaviors of the employees who were to operate in this new way.

The second position in the change model of Figure 8.1 is the need to *assess readiness for change*. Listed here as features are the urgency, top management support, key player analysis, change agent appraisal, and situational analysis. Clearly changes are more likely to fail without a perceived sense of urgency. Those who must implement the change and thereafter live with it will need to clearly feel the need to make it work. In our example of Six Sigma, once the training has started and work has been released to the group with the new approach, there will be almost no way to go back. Assessing top management support is also critical, since when the inevitable resistance to change comes up, they must stand firm and devote whatever resources are needed. Identifying the key players who will lead the change (as well as those most likely to resist) is equally important. Some changes will be extraordinarily difficult for

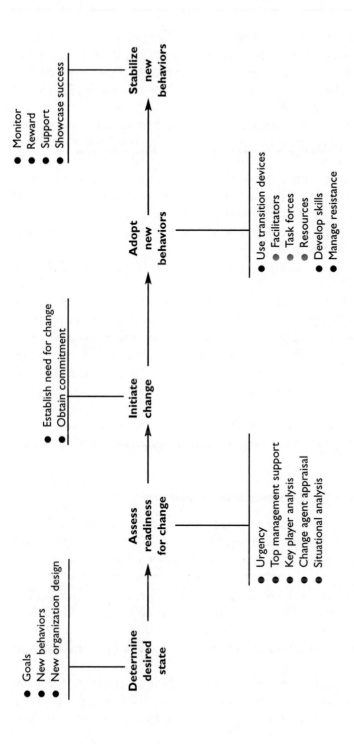

Figure 8.1 The change management model

Figure 8.1 comes from Professor Joe DiStefano at IMD, who adopted the ideas with permission from a set originally developed by Al Mikalachki, of the University of Western Ontario's Ivey Business School. The model is based on a large number of successful and unsuccessful changes.

certain people, and it is critical to not underestimate the problems that will be incurred. Finally, appraisal by the key change agent and analysis of the situation needs to be considered explicitly: Who is going to lead this, and how tough will it be—realistically? Can this person deliver the goods?

The third position or issue in Figure 8.1 is to be clear as to what it means to *initiate change*. This means no longer thinking about the change but doing it: Cut the umbilical cord and get it done. Establish the new operating processes and behaviors. Get performance in line with objectives. Sort out the individual issues. Supporting this activity is the clear establishment of the need to change: Why "we" must do this, what is expected of key people, and establishing their commitment to getting it done.

Then follows the need to institutionalize the change: *adopting new behaviors* for which execution can become routine, with no backsliding into former ways. As shown in Figure 8.1, this requires some degree of learning (and unlearning), perhaps using facilitators or task forces. New skill sets also need to be developed that allow optimization of the new approach. This position or stage in the model has risks. Errors can occur in learning/unlearning, and costs and other performance metrics are likely to be degraded in the short run.

Finally, Figure 8.1 depicts the need to *stabilize new behaviors*, develop best practices, modify reward systems, and showcase success.

Growing pairs of aces (Bombardier Transport)

The ideas in Figure 8.1 are relatively straightforward and familiar to most of us who read management literature. But developing pairs of aces is not a one-sided change process: The changes must be joint, coordinated, and collaborative. Let us now see how the changes indicated in Figure 8.1 would play out in the case of Bombardier Transport and its largest supplier, Knorr Bremse (KB). KB is best known for its braking systems, but it also makes train systems such as doors, air conditioning, toilets, and passenger information systems.

The desired state is a collaborative relationship or partnership, with a clear win–win for both parties. The immediate goal for BT was to reduce the costs for the components and systems it purchases from KB. A second goal was flawless execution, including perfect quality, and on-time delivery, but these are clearly not sufficient to establish a long-run partnership. Furthermore, these goals had to be explicitly matched with the goals on the KB side. As we have noted in other chapters, it amazes us how often customers fail to consider their suppliers' interests. The goals for Knorr Bremse were, first and foremost, that lower prices to BT did not come at the expense of their margins. Thus, the change agenda had to embrace joint cost-cutting, based on coordinated development of standardized products and modular approaches to design of braking systems.

For KB, reducing costs was an insufficient objective, and it was important for both firms to recognize this. Cost-cutting by itself would probably lead to long negotiations over who should get what proportion of the savings, as well as detailed part-by-part discussions. A second key objective for KB was to increase volume. Since the company already had the major market share in braking systems, it was looking for volume increases in other train systems, such as doors.

It is absolutely critical that these different and potentially conflicting sets of goals be made explicit. If this is not done, the desired state we defined above (a collaborative relationship/partnership) is just so much nonsense. The desired state can now be more sharply defined as initially a joint working process to create a catalog-based standard braking system approach, with a high degree of commonality, where either party can quickly calculate prices. However, this desired state could also jointly be seen as a condition that, when in place, supported significant development of new business activity. At the risk of redundancy, we want to stress yet again how important it is for this desired state to be made explicit and shared. In this example, it was necessary to follow through on the additional business when the standardization had been achieved.

Turning to the second issue in Figure 8.1, it is clear that readiness for change must be assessed in both firms. BT and KB each needed to believe that the way forward made sense, was worth the efforts that would be expended, was the best use of scarce resources, and should be pursued with urgency. This was not easy, since in both firms the assessment had to take place in several organizational units, each with their own perceptions and biases regarding the other firm. Thus, part of the situational analysis was to assess who and what organizational units would be most and least supportive of the desired state. Even more importantly, where was misalignment most likely to occur—and what would be done about it?

As mentioned in Chapter 1, a key activity occurred in a joint workshop with key executives from both firms. At an early point, a "time out" was called by the executives of KB and rapidly agreed to by BT. Each firm formed a caucus to definitively ask, "Do we really want to do this?" "Are we ready to sign on and carry it through?" "It is we who will have to do it!" This time out took almost one hour, but the result was agreement, along with a deeper understanding of what was required on each side— and jointly.

Initiating change is shown as obtaining commitment and establishment of a clear need for change. In this example, in addition to the "time out" session, we as third parties discussed their role with each side's most senior executives. This can work only if they definitively want it to work and commit to it. The real commitment from these executives came in stages. There was an original blessing of the activity, but about six months into the project, after some excellent results had been achieved, there was a subsequent meeting of the original group—plus the senior executives. The result was a deeper commitment, based on a solid foundation of trust and perceived win–win.

The most important new behaviors to be adopted are those that cross the two companies. In particular, the selling and buying processes have been vastly changed. There is no more negotiation and haggling over the detailed costs of every item in a braking system. The price is determined by the catalog, and it is clear that deviations from standard components and approaches will result in much higher costs. The result is combined emphasis on standard products, with predictable performance. All this results in greatly reduced work for both buying and selling.

Price negotiations now take a different approach. The key questions relate to total volume and combining of work across several contracts. If a brakes contract for a train series in France can be combined with the doors contract, then what reduction from catalog prices can be negotiated? If the contract for the train series in France can be coupled with one in England, what could be done here? This kind of discussion leads toward the "super-supplier" concept we developed in Chapter 1. That is, the two firms are working jointly to sweat KB's assets and finding ways to make this mutually advantageous.

Facilitation in adopting the new behaviors is a critical issue. In the case of BT and KB, there were two high-level executives who served as "godfathers" to these efforts. This involved the reduction of misalignment, as well as an ongoing dialog. No surprises became a key part of their working relationship.

The issue of *stabilizing behaviors* also needs to be seen in terms of the power of two. The benefits that each firm is receiving need to be clearly understood and communicated. The level of business between them is one key indicator, but so is the entire set of perceptions across the organization. BT and KB have implemented an online survey, based purely on perceptions, where key people are periodically asked their opinions about flawless execution (quality/delivery) as well as the four dimensions of our Rubik's cube in Chapter 7 (win–win, trust, misalignment, and strategy).

Finally, it is critical to understand that what BT and KB have achieved should be regarded as a beginning, not an end. The final objective should be pair of aces performance, which will require an ongoing set of transformative changes. In every case, we are talking about change management and the power of two. The changes must occur in both customer and supplier, and be jointly owned and jointly implemented.

Growing pairs of aces (ABB)

Another example we have examined in some depth is ABB and its development of global account management. We shall come back to the general topic of key/global account management shortly, but let us now quickly examine the interplay between ABB and Caterpillar using Figure 8.1.

The *desired state* on ABB's part was to increase its sales to Caterpillar from $50 million to $500 million. However, this was not remotely on the radar screen for the key Caterpillar executives when their joint efforts started. The much more mundane desired state for Caterpillar was to have a guaranteed supply of turbochargers for its large diesel engines, delivered on time, with perfect quality and predictable pricing. For ABB Turbochargers, the desired state was satisfying one of its top five clients while maintaining good margins on the business.

The *assessment for readiness for change* was possible only when a key group of Caterpillar executives started meeting with a similar group from ABB. There was significant need for reassessing the relationship, finding the reason why it was not as it should have been, determining what needed to be done, and who needed to do it. The steering group needed to meet periodically—and to develop a renewed sense of trust. As mentioned in Chapter 5, this required a copious quantity of red wine.

The necessary *changes were initiated* by task forces, composed of executives from both companies. They were charged with initiating the changes, producing concrete results, and reporting them to the steering group on a fixed schedule.

Adoption of new behaviors was a process that was less formal than it might seem, but the results speak for themselves. A key executive from each company again became a godfather for the joint organizational change process. They worked to overcome the resistance and to keep everyone focused on the key objectives, as they became known. Let's not make this sound too easy though: New attitudes and openness to others' ideas was critical.

Behaviors were stabilized on both sides. Flawless execution was achieved, and a long-term contractual relationship was established. The key executives said that they had no need to look at the contract. People in both companies knew how to make things work with no problems.

Finally, the ABB approach shifted to reach for the longer-term ABB desired state ($500 million). In this case, the ABB key global account manager for Caterpillar moved to Peoria, the site of Caterpillar's headquarters. There, his task was to first make sure that the existing turbocharger business proceeded with no problems, and look for new ways to make it better. Beyond this, he worked to get ABB turbochargers used on more of Caterpillar's engines, to facilitate joint R&D for Caterpillar's next generation of diesel engines, to find other ways that ABB competencies could be applied to Caterpillar's diesel engines (such as sensing and exhaust scrubbing), and finally to look for "white spaces" where ABB could adapt its products and talents to Caterpillar needs. In each one of these endeavors, the change management model of Figure 8.1 needed to be employed—jointly. ABB and Caterpillar needed to clearly see the benefits of joint work—the win–win.

From key account management to key collaboration management

Many companies see key account management and global account management as desirable states. Their goal is similar to that of ABB: to sell significantly more to existing customers. A move from $50 million sales to $500 million should be easier to achieve than implementing a $500 million acquisition. Unfortunately, key/global account management is too often seen as one-sided: what must *we* do to implement key account management? From the power of two perspective, the question is not what the seller needs to do but what the buyer and the seller need to do—jointly.

Classic issues in key/global account management

The literature on key account management largely focuses on the following key issues/dilemmas:

- What is the distinction between global account management and key account management?
- To whom should a key/global account manager report?
- Who should get credit for sales to global accounts? The GAM? Local sales organization? Division?
- How should we organize for KAM/GAM?
- How does GAM/KAM mesh with your matrix organization?
- Who in your company will resist the most? What are you to do about it?
- What are your customers demanding? To what extent are they globalized?
- Which customers are organized to buy globally?
- What are the IT issues associated with selling on a global basis?
- How do you select key or global accounts?

The typical resolution of these conflicting demands is to decide on the best organizational form to support key/global account management, and then bite the bullet. The alternative is to start with something less than optimal, with plans to migrate over time.

We see this issue as being as one-sided as that of change

management: Key/global account management must reflect what is best for the particular customer and supplier. Buying and selling should be jointly designed. Unfortunately, the optimal design will be unique to each customer–supplier pair. We come back to an earlier chapter in which we opted to sell the way the customer (each customer) wishes to buy. Moreover, you also must sell in ways that are possible to implement. If a company has a history of strong country management, it will be difficult to change it dramatically.

✔ It may be possible to teach an old dog some new tricks, but meowing is not one of them.

Finally, each key customer will have his or her unique situation, and it will be difficult to dictate a "one size fits all" approach to global/key account management. To think that ABB can use the same approach to Caterpillar as it does to ExxonMobil is naïve. In fact, the approach for ExxonMobil will need to be different from that for BP.

We see some fundamental problems in trying to decide the best approach to key/global account management. First, as just mentioned, customers have different desired states in working with a KAM. Second, if the goal is truly to move from $50 million to $500 million, it will require a lot more than some organizational reshuffle. What this implies is that those companies that start off by establishing 100 key or global accounts are not serious. Our rule of ten still holds. It may be OK to label many customers as key accounts, but developing pair of aces relationships needs to be limited to five to ten customers at a time. Each requires a very signif-icant investment of time, which should not be underestimated. Over time the number of key accounts can grow, and each individual rela-tionship needs to grow—and be tested. As we saw in Figure 8.1, the relationships can go up and down. Delisting of a key account has to be an expectation.

Then there is the issue of evolution. You should expect to change things over time. Going from $50 million to $500 million will require a continuing series of transformational changes. You need to start with where the action is, and then push the evolution—big time. The ABB–Caterpillar initial change agenda is in only one divi-sion, largely in one or two country organizations, and it comes to

ABB after abortive efforts to diminish the power of country organizations. All of this must be taken into account. You need to start with what is possible, focused on what makes sense for the particular organizational units involved (i.e. determine the true desired state), and create a win–win—not necessarily the ultimate win–win, but one that opens up new possibilities.

What all this means is that efforts to establish the optimal organizational approach to GAM/KAM are probably misguided. It needs a mass-customization mentality, it makes sense to start with whatever can be an agreed desired state between a customer and a supplier, that state needs to be as concrete as possible, and the change model of Figure 8.1 needs to be followed. Then, as always, the questions are: What is next? And what changes are needed to achieve it?

Longitudinal growth versus lateral growth

In the ABB–Caterpillar example, we see that new growth opportunities exist in selling more turbochargers to the existing Caterpillar buyers. This should be seen as longitudinal growth—desirable but fundamentally simpler than more complex extensions. Creating joint R&D for new diesel engine designs is still perhaps best labeled as longitudinal to Caterpillar. However, although these extensions may fall roughly into the same buying organization (diesel engines), they require new buy-in from new selling organizations. The engine sensing group may not have dealt with diesel engine issues. Its salespeople will be organized on a different basis, with different priorities and incentives. And there is an even bigger stretch for the smokestack-scrubbing experts to take on diesel engine emissions. From the ABB side, this enhancement of the business model needs to be seen as lateral.

Engine sensing and scrubbing are not easy (longitudinal) extensions of business inside ABB. They are better labeled as lateral extensions, with a clear understanding of the efforts and roadblocks involved:

- Will the engineers in the sensing and scrubbing units be willing to invest time in working with Caterpillar?
- Will their sales colleagues be interested in long-run "maybe" business?
- Do they view these efforts as charity for their turbocharger colleagues?

- What does the GAM need to do to motivate them?
- Has the long-run business impact for ABB been realistically defined?
- What is the roadmap to achieve a truly good result?

For ABB, selling to another division inside Caterpillar is perhaps a more significant case of lateral growth. Lateral growth needs to be understood and not underestimated in terms of the efforts required: Bringing another ABB division into Caterpillar's diesel engine business is probably an order of magnitude change from selling more turbochargers. But selling to another Caterpillar division is two orders of magnitude. And if this also involves a new division inside ABB, perhaps *three* orders of magnitude is more like it.

In every case, the application of Figure 8.1 to the joint changes required should provide a reality check.

It is far too easy to underestimate the change management requirements to achieve lateral growth. However, lateral growth is indeed what will be required to go from $50 million to $500 million. Figure 8.2 depicts the differences between longitudinal and lateral growth.

ABB and Caterpillar with traction motors

At one point, the ABB GAM residing in Peoria became aware of a Caterpillar new product initiative: a large mining machine that would be propelled by traction motors (like the Toyota Prius). ABB

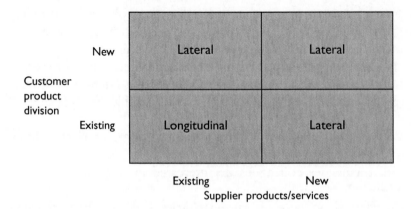

Figure 8.2 Longitudinal versus lateral growth

has two divisions that make traction motors, in Sweden and Italy, where they are manufactured for locomotives. This looked like a good chance to expand the ABB business with Caterpillar, so contacts were made between the two organizations. The possibility did not become a reality, and in retrospect it is easy to see why. The business would have required a significant investment in human resources by the Italian business unit (particularly engineering time), and it lacked the people to take on the project. It would also have mandated a major plant expansion, and at that time ABB was trying to shift plant investment from Europe to lower-cost countries. The Italians were also unsure whether Caterpillar was simply interested in another price quotation. Caterpillar, for its part, approached this potential business as a classic request-for-quotation exercise—not the way you treat a true partner. In the end, the Italian plant quoted with a relatively high price for a product with minor variations from its current production models. The business went to a competitor.

Missing this opportunity was too bad for both organizations. The total value of ABB products and systems that could have been incorporated into the mining machine was something like ten times the size of the traction motor contract. Entering another product division immediately would have set up ABB to work on longitudinal growth in this division. For Caterpillar, if it could have engaged in joint product design with ABB, there is a good possibility that the two could have created a superior product for the market, with win–win results.

Doing any of this requires more than a key or global account manager. He or she can establish good relationships with an existing customer buying organization; the lateral growth moves need more. In fact, what is needed is a set of godfathers in both companies that can jointly look for customer white spaces and untapped supplier competencies. They will need to jointly determine whether there is a long-term desired state that justifies investments on both parts. One part of that investment is to jointly go through a process such as that illustrated in Figure 8.1.

To some extent, this activity exists in most supplier organizations. For example, ABB's global account managers report to a senor manager at the executive board level, bypassing divisions, countries, and business units. But again, by itself this is clapping with one hand. The power-of-two payoffs come from collaborative efforts at all levels.

Where is the win–win?

The obvious question that arises from the traction motor example is: Why would Caterpillar want to do this? The company has a perfectly good buying organization (perhaps with some good rottweilers). It is executing a classic procurement approach: requests for quotation, evaluation, negotiation, award of contract, and so on.

In the final analysis, it is imperative that Caterpillar's godfather agrees with ABB's goal. That is, this person needs to believe that the $50 million to $500 million is in Caterpillar's best interest, and that ABB is one of the few suppliers with which Caterpillar should make the necessary investments. Is it realistic for ABB to expect this?

  ✔ Of course not—not the whole enchilada.

This must take place incrementally, where there is joint search for significant win–wins and continually demonstrated results. But make no mistake: the key metric for both ABB and Caterpillar is sales growth. This is the indicator that progress is on track. Caterpillar might start down this road with several suppliers, evaluating which ones are delivering the bacon. These are the ones where further investments of time and energy are warranted. The same applies to ABB: OK, have 50 or 100 global accounts, but keep track of which ones are embracing the power of two concepts and philosophy—and be prepared to delist.

A similar story exists for Bombardier Transport and Knorr Bremse. There too, the objective should include significant growth in sales for KB to BT. This implies ongoing gains in inter-firm operating efficiency, larger bundles of goods and services, growth in non-brakes business for KB, and joint work in emerging markets such as China. Again, this needs to be an evolutionary process, supported by the most senior-level executives.

Assessing the payoffs

The power of two journey needs guidance, a roadmap that can be updated in light of new conditions, a set of metrics to clearly demonstrate win–win, and a shared understanding of the evolutionary stages. Chapter 2 identified four distinct stages of collaboration: flawless execution, total cost of ownership, value/cost, and strategic alignment. These represent one way to conceive of the joint journey to pair of aces status. For ABB and Caterpillar, the clear original shared objective was to achieve flawless execution in turbochargers: guaranteed supply, on-time deliveries, and perfect quality for Caterpillar. For ABB, this flawless execution should yield detailed demand estimates and adherence to scheduled production at Caterpillar. These in turn should lead to predictable revenues, a clear sense of priorities, and stable workload requirements.

For BT and KB, the original BT goal is flawless execution in braking systems, routine use of standard braking components, and on-time deliveries, with no quality problems. KB is looking for better visibility into BT production planning systems, fewer changes, and on-time payment of invoices. Again, flawless execution is the base.

The next stage—in turbochargers—could be to jointly identify costs in either company that could be eliminated through better joint processes. These could be any of the issues we identified in our earlier discussion of total cost of ownership. Examples might include ABB taking on a greater role in after-sales service, particularly for diesel engines in large ships that might need repairs in places where ABB has better facilities than Caterpillar.

For BT and KB, TCO improvements might focus on reducing non-value adding activities such as documentation and detailed contract terminology. The two firms can also clearly develop trains with braking systems (and other systems) that require less down time and lower maintenance.

When moving on to value/cost, there is certainly a potential for ABB to help Caterpillar design new engines that will be more competitive, with lower fuel consumption and reduced pollutants. ABB could perhaps also help Caterpillar expand its product line, making an important contribution to the company's top-line growth.

Value/cost for BT and KB could include better entry and support of the Chinese market for trains, joint marketing to train operators, combined design efforts to create more effective braking systems or doors with fewer field failures, and a combined approach to support train maintenance.

Strategic alignment for ABB and Caterpillar might include combined engineering efforts to optimize airflow though a diesel engine designed to optimize that airflow, or even a combined effort to jointly enter new markets, such as through incorporating ABB robotics technology into new Caterpillar products. For BT and KB, an example might be to create a joint venture in China, or to deploy KB personnel in BT factories to install doors in ways that reduce after-sales service calls.

Rapid evolution is key

Any and all of the above are possible. The goal, when embracing the power of two, is to build on results as soon as they appear—do *more*, faster, and better. It is far too easy to become satisfied with interim results.

How do you start? Our advice is to begin with any problem perceived as important by both the customer and supplier—but one for which solving the problem is going to make a real difference. This problem, when solved, should lead to another opportunity, because the group who solved it will have new enthusiasm, and because there are always new horizons.

It is useful to assess whether the new opportunity is longitudinal or lateral, for both the customer and the supplier. Lateral problems are much more difficult, and require significantly higher efforts to move through Figure 8.1.

So what?

This chapter is in some ways an extension of Chapter 6, where the emphasis is on "delivering the bacon"—developing and nurturing pairs of aces. This chapter though is more of a manifesto: The best bet in developing your competitive advantage is in believing in the power of two—and trying your best to achieve it. Can you ever reach the state of dozens of pairs of aces? This result is doubtful, but we believe the pursuit of the objective to be in your best interest. You should pick the five to ten suppliers and five to ten customers for which true payoffs might be achieved.

It is important to not be naïve about how difficult the process will be, or to put your efforts into pairs with no hope of paying off. Once again, we implore you to not flog dead horses. If your marketing folks wish to label all kinds of customers as key accounts, global accounts, or empirical accounts, fine. But don't let such nonsense lure you into forging (and keeping) alliances that will not pay off.

So how do you tell? Rigorously applying the change model of

Figure 8.1 is good advice. The desired state needs to be absolutely clear and well stated, and must include a definitive win–win. Sloppy definitions of what is to be achieved can lead only to wasted efforts and poor results. The other issues in the model need to be equally well defined. Clear definition of the steps, the process to be followed, and benchmarks are well advised.

Finally, we recognize that what we provide in this chapter runs counter to much standard thinking about change management and key/global account management. Good!

Chapter 8 has been devoted to understanding the need for joint change—in order to obtain the power of two. In the end, there will be greater joint efforts than you would have expected, and it is important to not underestimate the efforts to make this a reality. In our final chapter, we turn to a more personal set of issues: How can you leverage the ideas in this book? And how can you realistically make a difference—in a reasonable time frame?

CHAPTER 9

Harnessing the power of two

We come now to the last chapter. Here we ask *you*—as a reader—whether the ideas we have presented make sense to you, and whether you would like to play a role in seeing them implemented in your company. If so, then we feel some obligation to help in whatever ways we can. Our experience indicates that the key requirement is to create enough belief in your organization to generate the necessary momentum for change. Changing people's lives is not easy. Development of collaborative relations necessitates changing closely held traditions and culture—the ways things are done—and, more important, the underlying reasons for doing so. We have seen many companies that can say the words "win–win," but meaning them is quite a different matter.

We divide our advice into two categories: driving the changes from procurement, and driving them from sales. Think carefully about the changes implied, how you might best be able to help with them, and where you might best form alliances to support your activities.

Driving from procurement

Clearly, one choice of where to start is whether this is to be from a purchasing point of view or from sales. In most companies, sales has a higher profile, is sexier, and has an easier time obtaining resources. On the other hand, we have noted at several points that salespeople are often surprisingly passive, do not wish to rock the boat, and would just as soon leave things as they are. In essence, it matters little whether you start with a customer or two or with a supplier or two. What does matter is that one or two is not 100, and clear objectives are formulated. To some extent, the choice depends on the company's existing strategy. If top-line growth is a key issue, then sales makes sense. If cost reduction and lower component costs are the key, then procurement is probably a better starting point.

The overall vision

It helps a great deal if someone—perhaps the chief procurement officer—believes in these ideas. However, "belief" realistically needs to be seen as conditional. You may find our ideas as appealing as motherhood and apple pie, but they are scary for many people. There will be considerable skepticism in your company—rightly so—whether any of this can work.

In one of our consulting assignments, there was a senior person who expressed great enthusiasm in terms of the ideas and their potential for the company. But in reality, he saw the project as potentially "radioactive": if it failed, he wanted to make sure it bore none of his fingerprints.

What all of this means is that commitment is going to be partial at best, with many reservations, plenty of skepticism, and reluctance to put personal prestige at stake. There will be a great need to achieve a quick win and to celebrate it strongly.

Establish a mafia

If you want to achieve results with these ideas, it is critical to establish a relatively small group that believes in the concepts and is willing to commit resources to making it work. This might be an informal group, acting without official sanction, but at some point it will need to increase its legitimacy, perhaps by getting collaborative efforts on the chief purchasing officer's list of strategic goals.

This group also needs to own the procurement effort—however it is scoped—and determine what needs to be changed in order for it to succeed. This implies applying the change management ideas of Chapter 8 and understanding how they will need to evolve over time. At the same time, this group must not get too far out in front. Sometimes the necessary changes need to be made obvious to a large group before they can be achieved.

Pilot a project

Establishing a pilot project is one excellent way to get started. By definition, a pilot is not expected to have a success rating of 100 percent. A pilot has the luxury of being able to bend the rules—that is, it is an experiment, so standard operating procedures can temporarily be dispensed with. But the pilot must be chosen carefully: It needs to be one for which the supplier is known to be cooperative and interested in making the plan work, where the supplier sees the pilot as in its long-term interest. Success should lead to a significant increase in business, a different position in your company's supplier segmentation model, etc. It is important that these goals for the supplier are indeed possible—not guaranteed—but that you genuinely wish them to happen. If this is not the case, the end result will not only be a lack of success, it will also lead to significant reduction in trust by the supplier and very tough conditions in your company for further collaborative efforts.

The pilot allows your company to start small, minimize the risks, and avoid creating a huge mandate for internal organizational change. On the other hand, if the supplier chosen is seen as trivial, it is harder to convince others of the benefits. At Bombardier Transport, one of the original five suppliers was Knorr Bremse, its largest supplier (and BT is KB's largest customer).

There is something to be said for the pilot including more than one supplier. In addition to the risk of putting all your eggs in one basket, there is the issue of comparing results, approaches, and success/failure. A small series of pilot projects gets more people involved as well.

Identify role models

A related issue concerns those dedicating their energies to making a pilot project a success. These people first need to be given the time and freedom to work on the project. Those who do deliver the goods must be given recognition for their efforts. Their actions need to be seen as the right way to support collaborative procurement, with others copying them—and unlearning other ways of working.

We believe it is useful to find a way to let people "blow off steam" about the supplier that has been chosen for the pilot. There will always be bad stories and rumors about a supplier, and it is not even important that they be true or false. The same is true for the supplier: people there will also remember the times your company played some bad trick on it. All of these tales should not be suppressed, but should be evaluated for present relevance. This typically results in: OK, now let's get on with it.

Driving from sales

Driving from sales is the obvious other choice. Many issues are the same. In fact, at some point it is useful to drive both ways and then ask why there are any differences. There shouldn't be: Collaboration is a two-way street.

In one recent case, we had achieved great success with suppliers, and many people in the company saw the potential for working in these ways with some key customers. But the salespeople declined to follow up on their professed enthusiasm with a commitment of resources: "That's a terrific idea, let's do something about it next year."

The question of number is also interesting here. If salespeople see this as a new endeavor in which some customers are to be given special treatment, surely they will want their customers to be given this special designation. That is how a company ends up with 100 key accounts.

The vision

Again, someone needs to take ownership for definitively increasing collaborative efforts with a few key accounts. The higher the place in the organization, the better. This also raises the question of how/who should choose the customer companies that will be targeted for collaborative efforts.

✔ You need to be careful about visions—they can easily become hallucinations.

The key here is to pay close attention to the dictates of Chapter 8. A clearly articulated win–win—one that is eminently feasible—is critical.

In some ways, it would seem that your company should carefully examine the potential customer partners in terms of their technical competence, existing level of business, potential for the future, growth, financial health, and so on. But experience indicates that readiness is a more critical issue:

- Is this customer in need of some major change?
- Might we be able to provide it?
- Can we pull this off in a reasonable time period?
- Does the customer see collaboration as a good idea or as a short-term way to get lower prices?
- Who is in fact trustworthy?
- Who wants to play this kind of game?

In our experience, the final choice is often made in a fairly ad-hoc way, but it has the buy-in of senior managers on both sides.

The group

We again see the wisdom presented above about the effectiveness of a mafia-type organization, one that operates with its own rules, and one that seeks forgiveness rather than permission. Change management will need to be seen jointly, in both the customer and the supplier, which necessitates an excellent working relationship. The mafia must be cross-company, and sometimes one group will need to go out of its way to help the other with its own internal issues.

Projects

Here we sometimes find ourselves embroiled in true "projects." The customer often has a need for much more than the items the company is selling: It needs the items included in an operating environment. In fact, it desires what the goods can create, rather than the goods themselves. This is a key issue for ABB, since increasingly, the company wishes to deliver turnkey projects, which might be automated factories, generating plants, or an offshore wind farm. In each of these cases, the new roles for collaboration are significantly altered, and ABB needs to find the best ways to deliver what is needed, with minimal recourse to legal documents. For these large projects, the customer and the supplier must work together in their best joint interests.

The individuals

Once again, there is a need for you to find those who can best work in cross-company projects. It is critical that they be appreciated and rewarded, and perhaps for you to protect them. It is also important that best practices be learnt, continuously improved, and repeated in other projects. These are particularly tricky when they are applied to joint work. It is not enough for a firm like ABB to learn how to do its own work, or even how to work with Caterpillar. It needs to understand how to develop collaborative project management as a core competence.

So what?

Now that you as a reader understand the power of two value that can come from developing a pair of aces, with either one of your suppliers or one of your customers, we hope you will make the necessary investment. The journey should be fun, it certainly will be exciting, and it can create stunning results. In the final analysis, however, the "so what?" in this chapter needs to be personal: What is in this for you? We believe strongly that the power of two ideas are real, they can be made to work, and they are a best bet for the competitive future of your company. But they will not come without the dedication, hard work, and the personal commitment of some key individuals who are willing to upset existing ways of working and common perceptions. Those who make them a reality should end up being rewarded. But anyone who thinks this is an easy road to travel is best advised to leave it alone. So, good luck—we wish you all the best!

BIBLIOGRAPHY

Amaral, J., Billington, C.A. and Tsay, A.A. (2004) "Outsourcing production without losing control," *Supply Chain Management Review*, November–December.

Anderson, J.C., Narus, J.A. and van Rossum, W. (2006) "Customer value propositions in business markets," *Harvard Business Review*, March.

Billington, C. (2002) "HP cuts risk with portfolio approach," *Purchasing*, February.

Billington, C., Cordon, C. and Vollmann, T.E. (2006) "Developing the super supplier," *CPO Agenda*, Spring.

Billington, C. Sandor, J. and Vollmann, T.E. (2006) "Talk a common language," *CPO Agenda*, Summer.

Bower, J.L. and Gilbert, C.G. (2007) "How managers' everyday decisions create—or destroy—your company's strategy," *Harvard Business Review*, February.

Buchel, B. (2005) "Creating joint value," *The Smart Manager*, February–March.

Carter, J., Closs, D.J., Dischinger, J.S., Grenoble, W.L. and Maxon, V.L. (2006) "Executive education's role in our supply chain future," *Supply Chain Management Review*, September.

Constantinou, M. (2005) "Seven imperatives for successful collaboration," *Supply Chain Management Review*, January–February.

Cordón, C. (2005) "Lessons of the Nissan steel crisis," *CPO Agenda*, Spring.

Cordón, C. and Vollmann, T.E. (1998) "Building successful customer–supplier alliances," *Long Range Planning*, October.

Cordón, C. and Vollmann, T.E. (1999) "Building a smarter demand chain," *Financial Times Mastering Information Management*, February.

Cordón, C. and Vollmann, T.E. (2002) "The next game in purchasing:

make yourself the most attractive customer," *IMD Perspectives for Managers*.

Cordón, C. and Vollmann, T.E. (2002) "Outsourcing: the need for a strategic focus," *Achieving Competitive Advantage Through Collaborative Partnerships*, Montgomery Research.

Cordón, C. and Vollmann, T.E. (2005) "Who's the fairest of them all," *CPO Agenda*, Autumn.

Cordón, C. and Vollmann, T.E. (2007) "Winning Together," *CPO Agenda*, Spring.

Cordón, C., Vollmann, T.E. and Heikkila, J. (1998) "Thinking clearly about outsourcing," *Financial Times Mastering Global Business*, February.

CPO Agenda Debate. (2007) "What are procurement's key challenges in the next ten years?" *CPO Agenda*, Autumn.

Dyer, J.H. (1996) "Does governance matter? Keiretsu alliances and asset specificity as sources of Japanese competitive advantage," *Organization Science*, June.

Economist Intelligence Unit (2007) "Collaboration: transforming the way business works," *Economist*, April.

Fischer, B. and Boynton, A. (2005) "Virtuoso teams," *Harvard Business Review*, July–August.

Fisher, M.L. (1997) "What is the right supply chain for your product?" *Harvard Business Review*, February.

Francis, J. (2007) "Team building with the SCOR model," *Supply Chain Management Review*, March.

Galbraith, J.R. (2005) *Designing the Customer-Centric Organization: A guide to strategy, structure, and processes*, Jossey-Bass, San Francisco.

Galbraith, J.R. (2007) *Designing Your Organization: Using the STAR model to solve five critical design challenges*, Jossey-Bass, San Francisco.

Gulati, R. (2007) "Silo busting: how to execute on the promise of customer focus," *Harvard Business Review*, May.

Hald, K.S., Cordon, C. and Vollmann, T.E. (forthcoming) "Towards an understanding of attraction in buyer-supplier relationships," *Industrial Marketing Management*.

Hammer, M. (2007) "The process audit," *Harvard Business Review*, April.

Hardt, C.W., Reinecke, N. and Spiller, P. (2007) "Inventing the 21st century purchasing organization," *McKinsey Quarterly*, October.

Hargardon, A., and Sutton, R.I. (2000) Building an innovation factory," *Harvard Business Review*, May–June.

Hofman, D. (2006) "Getting to world-class supply chain measurement," *Supply Chain Management Review*, October.

Hoover, W.E., Eloranta, E., Holmström, J. and Huttunen, K. (2001) *Managing the Demand–Supply Chain*, Wiley, New York.

Hughes, J. and Weiss, J. (2007) "Simple rules for making alliances work," *Harvard Business Review*, November.

Kim, W.C. and Mauborgne, R. (2005) *Blue Ocean Strategy*, Harvard Business School Press, Boston.

Kohlrieser, G. (2006) *Hostage at the Table*, Jossey-Bass, San Francisco.

Kumar, N. (1996) "The power of trust in manufacturer–retailer relationships," *Harvard Business Review*, June.

Kumar, N. (2004) *Marketing as Strategy*, Harvard Business School Press, Boston.

Lambert, D.M., Emmelhainz, M.A. and Gardner, J.T. (1996) "So you think you want a partner," *Marketing Management*, February.

Lambert, D.M. and Knemeyer, A.M. (2004) "We're in this together," *Harvard Business Review*, December.

Liker, J.K. and Choi, T.Y. (2004) "Building deep supplier relationships," *Harvard Business Review*, December.

Masters, Coco. (2007) "How Boeing got going," *Time*, 17 September.

McGovern, G. and Moon, Y. (2007) "Companies and the customers who hate them," *Harvard Business Review,* June.

Meyer, C. and Schwager, A. (2007) "Understanding customer experience," *Harvard Business Review*, February.

Miller, J.G. and Vollmann, T.E. (1985) "The hidden factory," *Harvard Business Review*, September–October.

Monczka, R., Trent, R. and Handfield, R. (2002) *Purchasing and Supply Chain Management*, Southwestern College Publishing, Cincinnati.

Minahan, T.A. (2005) "Five strategies for high-performance procurement," *Supply Chain Management Review,* September.

Nanni, A.J., Dixon, J.R. and Vollmann, T.E. (1992) "Integrated performance measurement: management accounting to support the new manufacturing realities," *Journal of Management Accounting Research*, Fall .

Nelson, R.D. (2004) "How Delphi went lean," *Supply Chain Management Review*, November–December.

Poirier, C. and Quinn, F.J. (2006) "Survey of supply chain progress: still waiting for the breakthrough," *Supply Chain Management Review*, November.

Reinecke, N., Spiller, P. and Ungerman, D. (2007) "The talent factor in purchasing," *McKinsey Quarterly*, No. 1.

Romano, A.M. and Finley, F. (2006) "How Ann Taylor put strategic sourcing on the management map," *Supply Chain Management Review*, October.

Ross, D. (2006) "The intimate supply chain," *Supply Chain Management Review*, July–August.

Schmenner, R.W. and Vollmann, T.E. (1994) "Performance measures: gaps, false alarms and the usual suspects," *International Journal of Operations and Production Management*, December.

Tompkins, J.A., Simonson, S.W., Tompkins, B.W. and Upchurch, B.E. (2006) "Creating an outsourcing relationship," *Supply Chain Management Review*, March.

Van Weel, A. and Rozemeijer, F. (2005) "Changing course," *CPO Agenda*, Summer.

Vandermerwe, S. (1996) *The Eleventh Commandment: Transforming to "own" customers,* Wiley, New York.

Vollmann, T.E. (1990) "Cutting the Gordian knot of misguided performance measurement," *IMD Perspectives for Managers*, No. 4.

Vollmann, T.E. (1996) "Transformation: the difference between domination and death," *Financial Times Mastering Management*, 22 January.

Vollmann, T.E. (1996) "Manufacturing planning and control systems: are your improvement efforts correctly focused?" *IMD Perspectives for Managers*, No. 4.

Vollmann, T.E. (1997) "A passion for manufacturing: flawless execution," *Financial Times Mastering Management,* December.

Vollmann, T.E. (2000) "Boundary-crossing networks," in Paul Strebel (ed.), *Focused Energy: Mastering bottom-up organization,* Wiley, New York.

Vollmann, T.E. (2000) "Turbo-kaizen," in Paul Strebel (ed.), *Focused Energy: Mastering bottom-up organization*, Wiley, Chichester.

Vollmann, T.E., Berry, W.L., Whybark, D.C. and Jacobs, F.R. (2005) *Manufacturing Planning and Control Systems*, 5th edn, McGraw-Hill, New York.

Vollmann, T.E. and Cordon, C. (1997) "Revitalizing restructuring: five imperatives for the future," *IMD Perspectives for Managers*, No. 8.

Wilkins, R.L. (2007) "Competitive intelligence: the new supply chain edge," *Supply Chain Management Review,* January–February.

Yip, G.S. and Bink, A.J.M. (2007) "Managing global accounts," *Harvard Business Review*, September–October.

INDEX

A

ABB
  Caterpillar key account
    management, 37, 40–3, 81,
    84–5, 102, 107–11, 140,
    142, 145, 159, 172–8
  pair of aces development,
    169–71
  top line growth, 2
Airbus, 47–9
attraction, 14, 55–9, 104–7
  ten golden rules for customers,
    58–9
  ten golden rules for suppliers,
    106–7

B

Babynov
  Huhtamaki, + Numico
    relationship, 10, 137, 139
benchmarking, 21, 32, 60, 99,
  119, 121–3, 149
Bombardier Transport (BT)
  benchmarking, 122–3
  cascaded collaboration, 52
  competitive advantage, 2
  improvement project, 9, 113,
    133–4, 137, 139, 140, 144
  pair of aces development,
    166–9
  standardization, 65, 139

supply base reduction, 82, 86–7
systems integration, 16
total cost of ownership (TCO),
  61, 71, 155–6
Bossard Group, 103

C

Canon
  Hewlett-Packard relationship,
    2, 25, 102, 140–1, 144
capacity utilization, 49
Carrefour, 103
Caterpillar, 37, 40–3, 81–5, 102,
  140, 142, 145, 159, 169–71,
  172–8
change management
  change management model,
    165
  changing two at a time, 163–80
  collaborative relationships, 17,
    146–8
  facilitation, 160
  farm club, 51
  four stages, 27–46
  limit of ten, 48
Collins & Aikman, 59–60
commodity business, 15
Compaq, 140
compliance versus collaboration,
  38
continuous improvement, 118

cost as passenger, not driver, 34
cost reduction, 16, 20
country disease, 100–2
customer relationship management
    (CRM), 156–7
Cypress Semiconductor
    Solectron relationship, 10, 11,
        19

D
Danone, 11
deep dive, 132–3

E
e-auctions, 49
ERP systems, 127–9
Ethan Allen, 142
Ethiopian Airlines, 114

F
flawless execution
    ante to play, 62
    collaboration, 32
    defined, 29
Flextronics
    developing Microsoft Xbox, 11
    logistics, 15
Ford, 18, 59–60, 122
four stages of collaboration, 27–46
Freqon, 115–16

G
General Electric, 86
General Motors, 11, 12, 59, 64
Givaudan, 12
governance, 42, 159–60
Graham Packaging, 11

H
Hewlett-Packard
    Canon relationship, 2, 25, 102,
        140–1, 144
    source development, 23

top line growth, 38, 150
Honda of America, 1, 18–19, 49,
    140, 144, 149
Huhtamaki
    Babynov + Numico
        relationship, 10

I
IBM, 15
ICI, 95–7
Ideo, 132
implementation, 102–10, 146–60,
    163–80, 160

J
Johnson & Johnson, 122
Johnson Controls, 30
joint improvements, 20
just-in-time, 30–2

K
key account management, 81–5,
    107–10, 151–5, 171–8
Knorr-Bremse, 65, 144, 166–9

L
Lafarge, 70
leadership, 117, 158–9
Lear, 30
Lenovo, 160
life cycle costing, 35
longitudinal versus lateral growth,
    173–8

M
Mabe Estufas, 86
marriage analogy, 116–17, 141
Mattel, 38
Mazda, 122
measures
    moving beyond unit cost, 88–9
    perception based, 42, 65–6,
        109–10, 118–20

service levels, 30
should cost, 60
supply chains, 124
misalignment, 145–6

N
negotiation, 120–1, 146–7
Nestlé, 38, 100, 103–4, 146–7
network mapping, 130–1
Nissan, 81
Nokia, 21, 36, 53–5, 143, 144
NordAlu, 115–16
Numico
    Babynov+ Huhtamaki
        relationship, 10, 137, 139
    R&D with suppliers, 37, 150–1
    supplier support, 57

O
ombudsman, 43–4, 160
open books, 33, 75
outsourcing, 38
overall equipment effectiveness
    (OEE), 57

P
pair of aces
    at ABB, 169–71
    at Airbus, 48
    at Bombardier, 166–9
    defined, 2, 14, 51
    developing, 113–36
Partek, 24, 97
partnership, 85–6, 93, 148–9
perceptions, 28, 42, 65–6, 109–10,
    118–20
Peugeot, 49
power of two
    defined, 1, 160–1
    payoff, 16
Procter & Gamble, 19, 32, 51,
    127–9
procurement

driving point for transformation,
    181–4
restructuring, 47–68
Publicis, 59–60

R
Reckitt Benckiser, 87–8, 160
reverse purchasing, 74–6
Rockwool, 24, 97
rottweiler approach to purchasing,
    17
round robin, 131–2
Rubik's cube of partnerships,
    138–9, 149, 150, 151

S
sales
    driving point for transformation,
        184–6
    proactive approach, 91–112,
        150–1
    selling how customers want to
        buy, 69–90
segmentation
    customers, 14, 76
    selling to customer segmentation
        models, 76–81
    suppliers, 51
shared values, 21, 143
should cost measures, 60–1
Skanska, 24, 97
smart partners, 14, 55, 98–100
Solectron
    Cypress relationship, 10, 19
Sony, 15
standardization, 64–5, 100, 103,
    124–5
strategy, 143–4, 182, 184–5
super supplier
    defined, 1, 17
    Honda of America example,
        18, 143, 149
supply chain, 35, 49, 124, 127–9

Supply Chain Reference Model (SCOR), 123
systems integration, 34, 155–6

T
ten partners, 9–26, 43
Tetra Pak, 99–100
Texas Instruments, 36
top line growth, 38
total cost of ownership (TCO), 28–9, 52–3, 61, 103, 155–6
tough love for suppliers, 62–4
Toyota
    cost advantage, 1, 34
    supplier collaboration, 31
transformation process, 129–34, 168
transparency, 33
trust, 28, 138, 141–3
two-sided staircase, 124–7

U
Unilever, 12, 64–5, 95, 100–1, 109
unlearning, 26

V
value/cost, 36, 40, 69–70
Volkswagen, 30

W
Wal-Mart, 19, 32, 51
win–win, 50, 138–41
workshop, 24, 129–34, 168

Y
Yorozu America, 11

Z
Zara, 122